To
Professional Drivers
&
Parents &School Administrators
&
Teachers & Coaches

For
All Bus Passengers
&
especially
School Children & Youth
&
Their Bus Drivers

THE

GREATEST

SCHOOL BUS

DRIVER

EVER

~GARY HEINS~

THE GREATEST
SCHOOL BUS DRIVER
EVER

by GARY HEINS

Published by:

SWINGIN' G BOOKS
PO Box 784
Saint Johns, Arizona   85936

LCCN 2009 934475

ISBN   1-882369-52-1   #

DISCLAIMER:

This book is a highly-opinionated treatise on the subject of hauling people around where they need and want to go--it is not intended to over-ride the fine materials written by State Driver License Bureaus, State Departments of Transportation, State Motor Vehicle Departments, and State School-Bus Advisory Boards where professional drivers get much of their training, licensing, endorsements, and certification.

While this book is written *for* the children, . . . it is *not written to* the children. If you have trouble with the idea of free speech, you might think twice about getting on my bus--er, getting in my book. If you're going to leave this book laying around where minors might get ahold of it, you might consider high-lighting parts of it . . . with a black marker.

"All Routes . . . Revisited."

THE
GREATEST SCHOOL BUS
DRIVER EVER

\#

Motives For Writing This Book

Riiinnnng! Riiinnnng! Riiinnnng! It was my home telephone ringing, and I looked at my alarm clock and it was barely past 4 o'clock in the morning. Not too many people know my home number, and I got worried that the local school district was in need of another substitute driver. Normally, at the time, I didn't go to work until after 10am, because I'd recently landed a State job hauling pre-schoolers to Head Start, so it was easy for me to stay up late at night writing or at least watching the Westerns Channel. I dreaded having to sub for someone else so early in the morning and on such late notice. But I picked up anyway: "Yeah?"

"Gary, it's Nancy. I'm sorry to wake you, but I think you need to write a book about School Bus Driving. I've got to head to work soon, but I couldn't wait to tell you. That's the only way you're going to get any respect with your job. You're such a good writer, and you're just the man who could pull such a thing off. Go back to sleep, and I'll talk to you later. Bye."

. . . It took me a minute to realize what just happened, but she was right--I remember threatening to write such a book in the past, and that's probably where she got the idea from. I got up for a minute to let the cat in, and I remembered: "Gosh, I've written plenty of books--about horse wrangling and ski teach-ing,--but the only way they are going to sell . . . is if I write a much more needed book . . . about the *Greatest School Bus Driver Ever*. At least there ought to be a few thousand school bus drivers who would buy it. Who knows? Maybe then I could even quit my job as a school bus driver.

I climbed back in bed and made sure my alarm was set for 9am and tried to go back to sleep, fully aware the phone could ring yet . . . to sub a morning route for the regular schools.

If you think you know already what's in this book, I feel sorry for you. We aren't going to get stuck in traffic talking about the same old fundamentals of driving you should know before you even get your Driver's License. Good writers don't write books where you already know what's in it; we write infor-mation that may surprise you and be a lot more inter-esting than you thought--otherwise, why write the darn thing? We write about a subject to learn more ourselves. We as Americans are supposed to get a good basic education in twelve years of public school plus kindergarten, but I believe there is a percentage of us who just do their time and graduate . . . without ever really learning how to think for the real world. From kindergarten through high school, there are good teachers, and there are not-so-good teachers; the younger we are, the less we may know which is which--no, that's not right: the more help we need, the less we know how good a teacher is. The younger the stu-dent, the more important their teachers; or, the older and more mixed-up the student, the more important their teachers. . . . Because of the simple fact that most students don't go to school to be driven around in traffic all day, most school-bus driving jobs are part-time, and we all know that part-time jobs usually pay less per hour; . . . and, **because most school-bus driving jobs are part-time, most school bus drivers have to have a life separate from their school-bus life, in order to survive.** . . . School bus drivers are a diverse bunch . . . and a rare breed. . . . Sometimes, the best teacher a kid has . . . is his school bus driver--I should hope not the worst.

First off, I don't claim to be the Greatest School Bus Driver. I happen to be a School Bus Driver who is also a writer. --No, actually, I am a writer who is also a school bus driver--I have probably as many miles on the pen as I do in the buses. Well, I may not be a writer you've ever heard of; but, then again, have you ever met a famous school-bus driver?--we may get one of those yet, because of this book.

With that, we do care about who drives our kids to and from school--or we should care, and sometimes I wonder by some people's behavior concerning school buses. Did you ever find yourself out in the cold waiting for your school bus when you were a kid? Or, now that you're an adult, maybe you have worried about your kids waiting for a late school bus. Or maybe you've waited for the kids riding home to get dropped off way too late. Well, I'll tell you what: this book is a lot more overdue--decades overdue. School Buses can run late--in the name of Safety,--but sometimes they run late because of poor planning or poor logistics: a regular route driver may drive too fast for years; and then, the day to substitute takes over, he's unnervingly late. The terrible thoughts that go through parents' minds when they think their kids' school bus may be in trouble.

As a seasoned Ski Instructor in the winter . . . and a gruff horse wrangler in the summer, I have driven school buses off and on in a number of different states on most types of routes imaginable. Most recently, I have been driving for some of the youngest clients possible, 3-5-year-old pre-schoolers of the national program of Head Start--it is not surprising that these kids don't see me as "just their driver"; they call me "Teacher." You cannot imagine "the routes I have planted" in the school-bus business. I have developed strong opinions about what it means to be a school-bus driver.

I guess I was lucky to have some great teachers about the school-bus business early on in my career: their routes, grafted with my current routes, have made for some interesting observations. The best school-bus drivers have similar habits, common denominators. There are right ways to drive a route, and then there are ways that are not so right: I learned early on that . . . any route in the country ought to be designed and driven day-in and day-out so that any substitute driver can hop in the seat and do the same route on pretty much the same schedule--the substitute arrives at each drop point, just the same as the regular route driver, and the parents never have any thoughts of worry.

Originally, when I thought of writing about the Greatest School Bus Driver Ever, I realized there must be thousands of great school-bus drivers--well, there should be dozens anyway--or there ought to be more than one. This book is written for several reasons: first, I write it for the Safety of the kids; second, I write it for the vast array of drivers, to commend the good drivers

. . . and maybe to correct the not-so-good drivers; third, I write it for the rest of the adult population, so that they may better understand and respect and appreciate the school transportation operations . . . and the rare breed of folks who are driven to become school-bus drivers.

Maybe I am writing this book for revenge--yes, **RE-VENGE**: I've always tried to see school-bus driving as a profession, and I've been laughed at for thinking so. One of my best friends back around 1990 told me school-bus driving is too low of a goal and one of the dumbest jobs I could shoot for--how do you parents like that perception hauling your kids around? One of my bosses went so far as to say, there's so little to the job, you know everything you're ever going to know by the first few weeks, and there's no reason for yearly pay increases for experience.

In fact, after two years at Head Start in 2007, I was still making the same as a first-year driver, under $12per-hour, though the pay scale said I deserved $19 with my experience--$12 ain't bad for a first-year driver, but it's kind of an insult to an umpteen-year driver. Meanwhile, the administrators were getting hefty raises and driving around in new late-model government vehicles, while the bus they issued me was twelve years old, and it was like pulling teeth to get already-budgeted money for routine maintenance. When I was sent to two annual Heat Start conventions, paid for with our tax dollars, not one syllable was uttered concerning how the school buses link up with the rest of the program--remember, these are preschoolers 3- to 5-years-old we're talking about, with siblings running around the buses even younger, and it seems to me school-bus safety, or pedestrian safety, should be one of Head Start's highest priorities, more urgent than nutrition, heights-n-weights, or learning the ABCs. When they did my annual review of job performance, there was not even a box for the all-important Post-Trip Inspection, where you check for stowaways or sleeping kids on your bus after each run--kids can die real quick at that age if you leave them on the bus at high-noon in the hot sun . . . or over-night in the cold. It's frustrating and unnerving for school-bus drivers to be bossed around by people who don't even know what the job is and who aren't even licensed, certified, endorsed, or qualified to do it themselves.

At the beginning of my last school year with Head Start, they had me come to work two full weeks before the kids would arrive. I had my bus ready, my paper-work ready, and I was gung-ho to have that bus rolling on day one, to serve those kids and parents. But the higher ups in this state-government federally-funded agency told me they weren't ready for the bus to run; they said it was normally two weeks after school started before their Head Start buses would be rolling, a full month after all the employees reported for work-- because of government red-tape and paper-shuffling. I was embarrassed to tell the families and kids their bus wasn't running; meanwhile, the preschool teachers and their assistants and the lunch workers were all de-lighted to have their bus driver available for their vari-ous chores . . . like washing dishes, vacuuming the floor, everything but bus-driving and bus-related chores. More subtle was this big fact: when a pre-school bus rolls, it is required to have an adult monitor ride along with the driver, for several reasons involv-ing the health and safety of the little ones; so, if a bus wasn't rolling, this was a few hours a day less that the teachers or their assistants had to do. The frustration of going weeks not getting to do what I was hired to do . . . and the frustration of being questioned every time I did do my job, involving safety, custody, emergency preparedness--these are what finally drove me out of Head Start within a two-year period. For the record, I noticed the driver before me had only lasted a year, and the driver after me lasted one year--and this is not the worst-paying thirty-hour-week job with full benefits. To make a long story short, I can think of several Head Start preschools in one state . . . where they don't even have a bus driver anymore--because the higher-ups and coworkers don't know how to respect them and let them do their job.

Sometimes I feel like people see me as the Barney Fife of school-bus driving, but: no! I'm the Wyatt Earp of school-bus driving, just like I'm the Wyatt Earp of ski teaching. I'm sorry, but people who think it's silly of me to approach School-Bus Driving as a profession are just flat out ignorant--God forgive them, for they have their head -- ----- ---. Remember, I'm not writing this to the kids but to the adults . . . for the kids . . . and the adults. I'm in charge here, so sit down.

(I swear they drive me to drink. I can't drive a school bus after a couple of beers; but I can work on writing this book after a couple of beers. --Would you like one? Maybe reading this book would be easier for you if you crack one open. In the writing and reading of this book, there are No Holds Barred. As I write this, it's January 19, 2009, Inauguration Eve--one would hope that **Honesty is the Best Policy** once again finally. Anyway, I don't have to drive tomorrow until late in the afternoon.)

Someone could make a whole blockbuster movie

about the School-Bus business, just full of outlandish entertaining humor, but no one dares make it because of the repercussions--it could cause death and mayhem for kids and drivers for years to come. They've made movie spoofs about Ski Patrol and Police Academy and Ski School, and there was Animal House about Greek Life at College, . . . Smokey and the Bandit about over-the-road truck driving; but School Buses seem to be off-limits because it would take a lot of careful talent to pull it off without getting a bunch of kids hurt or killed afterward. About the closest thing we've seen is a school bus in a Dirty Harry movie, but that wasn't a comedy, and unfortunately the school-bus driver was portrayed as an incompetent victim--I wouldn't mind seeing Dirty Harry as a substitute school-bus driver.

"Routes of Passage"

I don't claim to be the greatest school bus driver ever; but I do claim to be the best candidate to write the book about it. I am the only one to think of the title, and it's a book that's long overdue, more disturbing than a late school bus. Then, because I have been a seasonal mobile worker, a horse wrangler most summers . . . and a ski instructor most winters since 1979, intertwined with my career as a professional driver, I have probably had the opportunity to work for more school districts and bus outfits than most professional drivers combined--so I've seen what goes on in the school-bus business in more parts of the country than maybe any other driver. I should probably at least be nominated for a "Mobile Prize." . . . Part of what grates on me is this: . . . I happened to start at one of the best school districts when I was new to the school-bus business in the mid 1980s, Teton County School District in Jackson

Hole, Wyoming, . . . and Transportation Director Knowles Smith and his team of JoAnn Camenzind and Bear McKinney taught me most everything I needed to know, and they taught me right and the reasons why the first time--they are my idols in the School-Bus Business; I have taken this high standard with me to every district or company or agency I've worked for, and, I'm sorry to say, it hasn't been recognized or welcomed with open arms. So I do have a few battle scars, but there's no reason every driver should have to suffer the same old way.

So I started driving school buses in the fall of 1985, to complement my careers in horse wrangling and ski teaching. The Transportation Director there in Jackson believed I would be a good candidate for the school bus business because I had driven lots of big horse trailers, often-times with unruly rodeo broncs. I remember the Wyoming Autumn leaves matching the paint of my assigned bus--I took that as a sign. I had my own route for three years there in Jackson Hole, the thirteen-mile drive to Teton Village, the base of Jackson Hole Ski Area, "The Big One." The unique thing about my first bus route was this: since it was the road to North America's steepest, toughest, rowdiest destination ski area, still known for its frontier justice, my bus suffered more civilian red-light violations than all the other routes combined--the motorists, aggressive male skiers many, were on vacation, and school buses were the last thing on their mind. As a regular driver there, I drove as many field trips and activity trips as anyone--it was on a rotation basis, and Knowles was fair about it. . . . When I didn't have my own route there in Jackson Hole, for an additional few years, I substituted any of the routes. What I loved about working for Knowles

Smith was he backed every move or decision I made--
kids' or parents' bad behavior was dealt with, and red-
light violators were fined or prosecuted. . . . I took a
route in Bozeman, Montana, later years ago . . . where I
didn't stay three months because of the lack of support
disciplining the kids' bad behavior on the particular
route I was assigned, not to mention the lack of compensation for some of the necessary work performed,
like the mandatory daily pre-trip bus-inspection.

For about six years, for Texas-NewMexico-
&Oklahoma Coaches from 1996 to 2002, I drove the big
over-the-road forty- and forty-five-foot buses extremely heavy during the warmer half of the year,
sometimes well over six-hundred miles a day--with
fifty-some people on board, that can be a challenge for
even one day, . . . let alone day-in-n-day-out, month-
after-month, or year-after-year. I was what they called
an "extra-board driver," someone who would go anywhere at any time on maybe an hour's notice. Stationed out of centrally-located Pueblo, Colorado, I substituted and doubled line-runs linked with Greyhound
. . . between Cheyenne and Albuquerque or El Paso . . .
and Grand Junction and Wichita . . . and Denver or
Colorado Springs and Amarillo or Dallas. But, probably more than half the time, I drove charter buses
through twenty-four states, with every kind of group
imaginable: Boy Scouts from Kansas City, Missouri, to
Cimarron, New Mexico, and back; old folks to Laughlin, Nevada, or Branson, Missouri, and back; the U.S.
Army or Marines from Fort Carson, Colorado, to Fort
Bliss or Fort Hood, Texas, or Fort Irwin, California, or
Fort Smith, Arkansas, or Fort Sill, Oklahoma, or
Guernsey, Wyoming, or Pinon Canyon, Colorado; a
bachelor party from Fort Collins, Colorado, to Las Ve-

gas, Nevada; grade-schoolers to the Denver Zoo, middle-schoolers to the Museum of Natural History, high-schoolers to a junior college in Prescott or to cadaver-lab in Phoenix. I've had bus-loads of Promise Keepers for days at a time, wondering if I were "saved"; I've driven World War II veterans to their reunions, World War II Japanese Americans to their former prison camps; I've driven college athletic teams to their games, I've been to a lot of NFL football games, Major League Baseball, NBA basketball, the list goes on and on.

One thing unique about working for TNM&O Coaches (by the way, a less-dedicated driver would say simply "TNMO," while a more dedicated one would be sure to include the tricky extra word "and," hence "TNM&O"): when I started with them in 1996, all of their buses, MCIs, were manual transmissions, mostly seven-speed sticks--it takes several months to more than a year to get good at those things, and most professional drivers will tell you they are more difficult to shift than a semi-tractor, partly because the engine and drive-axle are clear in the rear of the bus, which can be like playing "Post-Office" with the transmission because of the driver and the clutch and the stick . . . being way up front. I took pride in how smooth my shifting got, and passengers often noted the difference--with other drivers, they could hear some grinding going on. In fact, most big bus companies like Greyhound prefer automatics, because not every driver can get the hang of a seven-speed stick. TNM&O is a subsidiary of Greyhound, and the buses paint job is the same, only it won't say "Greyhound" on the side, it'll say "TNM&O." When I left the company in 2002, they were converting to all automatics as well, because of the lack of talent--every year they would find more transmissions with broken teeth. Anyway, a stick shift is fine out on the open road, but it can be hell stuck in Denver traffic--you can wear out your left knee or the arch your left foot. I always used to tell the passengers, "They give the best bus to the worst driver . . . the worst bus to the best driver--that's how they balance things out," . . . to which they would always ask, "Is this the best bus?" . . . to which I would always smile and reassure them, "No, this is the worst bus."

The **Long Shortage of School Bus Drivers**

It's common knowledge that there is a chronic shortage of school-bus drivers, and there has been for many years. Several factors contribute to this problem: the qualifications are fairly stringent, the ability to care about and handle a bunch of screaming kids is not for everybody, the comparatively low-pay drives a lot of people away, and the ever-present lack of respect from all angles toward school-bus drivers is a huge deterrent. Let's examine each reason in detail.

School-Bus Drivers have several hoops to jump through before they are authorized to haul school children, let alone any kind of passengers. First, you need a CDL (Commercial Driver's License) class B or A--class B means basically big buses and straight trucks, while a class A allows you to move all the way up to semi-tractors-n-trailers. Then you need a Passenger Endorsement, and then you still need a Stop-Arm or School-Bus Endorsement, hence CDL-B-PS. Then you are required to pass a Department of Transportation (DOT) Physical. From there, you go through an extensive background check and get a State-Issued Fingerprint Clearance Card. Then you need a First-Aid/CPR

Card. . . . Oh, one more thing: you have to pass a Urinalysis Drug Test--this is what weeds out a whole bunch of prospects.

They can test a commercial driver for drugs just about any time they please, pre-employment, post-accident, annual, random, and so on. I think I've been tested as many as five times some years. One day, while driving a lumber delivery truck for a couple of months at a small lumber yard in Colorado about 1995, my supervisor thought I was having too much fun on the job, so he made me go take a pee-test a few blocks down the street over my lunch period. A lot of drivers would have been extremely upset, but I thought it was funny as all-get-out, knowing I was innocent and seeing the bewildered look on his face when the test results came back in my favor--maybe you haven't guessed, but I like to have fun while I'm working, as long as it doesn't interfere with the job, and in fact it can make a job easier to do.

Some people have a misguided notion that semi drivers are bigger and better than bus drivers, but I beg to differ--they are separate but equal: it's true a class B bus driver cannot hop in the seat of a semi-tractor-trailer, . . . but a semi driver cannot hop into the seat of a bus either without that P on his license. Then, when you look at the turn radius of a 40- or 45-foot bus, it is very similar to the turn radius of hinged eighteen-wheeler with a 48- or 53-foot trailer; but, remember, the eighteen-wheelers spend more time on the big open road and going in and out of big loading docks, while big buses with people from all walks of life get in some very tight places with low over-hangs and bottoming-out possibilities, like churches, restaurants-galore, hotels, you-name-it--and a lot of groups are notorious for telling a driver he's three-inches too far away from the curb. However, I will give you this: the toughest guys on the planet are those local-delivery truck drivers who back into the narrowest allies or heavy-traffic convenience stores and then have hundreds of cases of bottled beer to unload up-n-down steps through narrow doorways with people all around.

The next reason for the shortage of school-bus drivers is **the knack it takes to handle a bus-load of kids**. Junior High kids, about 7th, 8th, and 9th grades are about the toughest or trickiest age to handle--they will test you till you're in tears or almost ready to pop, if you let them,--and it's important to get total support from the administration, the parents, and other drivers involved with the same difficult kids. Middle-schoolers about 3rd, 4th, 5th, and 6th grades are pretty easy, but it helps if you know how to relate to them or make the bus ride interesting for them: I grab the PA mike and tell them I'm their "tour guide" and start pointing out all the interesting sites along the way; or I tell them "the bus ride is free, but it's 50cents to get off." I told one middle-schooler how, when I was a kid, I had to walk to school, "up-hill both ways," and he spent the whole bus route trying to figure how that could be possible. High-Schoolers 10th, 11th, and 12th grades are usually a pleasure, until you get one that's been mismanaged by other adults elsewhere in society--then you might have a real dangerous situation on your hands, as they can be bigger and stronger than a bus driver, you could be out-numbered, and there could even be knives or guns to consider nowadays. With the older kids, when I had my own route, I used to give them a Quote-of-the-Day over the PA system, some of which were my own, careful to remind them they don't have to agree with it.

When I had a group of high-school students out on a spring clean-up party one day, picking up trash on a country road, I called out a few BINGO numbers over the PA's exterior speakers, just for fun. A lot of you might disagree with my using the PA system for fun, but let me tell you: kids behave a lot better if they've got a fun and relaxed atmosphere--you don't want them to cringe and feel guilty every time the PA mike-button gets squeezed.

Elementary 1st and 2nd graders are a joy, but you have to be more careful for them, and you can have a high-pitched riot on your hands in a hurry if you don't have the knack, kind of like Arnold Schwartzenhager in *Kindergarten Cop*--it helps if you know each other. Kindergarteners are always in a lot of danger, because they have a lot to learn yet about pedestrian safety, and sometimes what they have learned so far from others may not be accurate for true safety. For a local mother-type who knows these elementary kids and kinder-gartener, this can be pretty easy, but danger can creep in if you let yourself get too complacent. For a substi-tute who doesn't know the kids, these younger kids can be one of the toughest and most-responsible gigs in school-bus driving.

I need to talk about Pre-Schoolers and even tod-dlers for a minute. I've mentioned I had a job with the national program of Head Start for 3-to 5-year-olds. I guess it was a state-run nationally-funded program, and the government red-tape and bureaucracy not only pretty much did me in, it at times put the children as risk. The reason I bring this up now is because . . . what happens in pre-school can help or hinder a kin-dergartener a year later. It was a six-hour a day job, where I drove the bus routes less than three hours a day, but I was supposed to use the remaining three hours to do a lot of other bus-driver stuff--like keeping accurate medical records and custody papers on every bus-kid, as well as maintaining and cleaning the bus, and instructing the young parents and teachers about pedestrian safety for this most-vulnerable innocent age. Now, state or federal law requires you have all this paperwork and a monitor to ride along to ensure the safety; when we did a pick-up or drop-off, we usually pulled clear off the road, clear in to the driveway, where the authorized parent or guardian was required to sign each kid on or off the bus. I don't believe in picking-up and dropping-off pre-schoolers out on a regular road or city street using the stop-arm, because these stops take more time because of the signing-in-n-out, and maybe the monitor/teacher needs to talk to the parent about an upcoming bake-sale or something. Well, at the end of a kid's last year at Head Start, the teachers and administrators thought it would be a wonderful idea to give the bus-kids an award for learning how to ride a bus safely--and I cringed. One has to realize: a small twelve-seat pre-school bus equipped with a monitor and pulling off the road for sometimes a few minutes . . . is a far cry from a big eighty-passenger bus out in the middle of the street or high-way that uses the stop-arm to control traffic that is not one-hundred-percent guaranteed controllable--to give these kids an award for "Mastering School-Bus Safety" was to tell everyone a lie, the kids and the parents and even other drivers. I knew how serious my job there was, but it was cut-n-dried, and all it was was a lift to and from pre-school--it wasn't meant to be some exclusive club to make the non-bus-kids feel left out. Getting run-over is one of the biggest causes of death for 3-to 5-year-olds, and it doesn't happen with eighteen-wheelers on the Interstate, it happens mostly right in their own driveway with the family station-wagon, or just outside a school-bus during loading and unloading. The parents and teachers often thought I was too much of a hard-ass when I suggested they shouldn't double-park their car like a UPS truck with the motor running and a 2-year-old toddler running loose in the car. Complacency has killed more people than we will ever know--and, if you can imagine the scenarios I'm touching on, even grown men aren't safe when being blind-sided by a barely-moving two-ton car driven by a 2-year-old.

The next reason for the chronic shortage of school-bus drivers is the **low pay** and usual **lack of benefits**, compared to other jobs of equal value. Moist people don't think there's anything to school-bus driving--they're all wet, they see it as "child's play." They see the trucks out on the Interstate hauling beer and toilet paper as more important, so they get more money for the work they do. (I guess I do have a dry sense of humor.) The low-pay hurts even more when you con-sider that school-bus route drivers usually have a split shift, so they have to show-up for work twice a day.

One time, driving a casino bus at 2-am, I refused to haul an unruly intoxicated gambler who'd lost a lot of money at Texas Hold'Em; the casino manager wrote a long letter explaining why I should be fired from the bus company, explaining, "It is my understanding that this driver's previous experience is limited to nothing more than school buses," flat out saying that school buses are nowhere near as important as flashy casino buses. I had to laugh, and DOT laughed with me. I let off some off-duty police officers halfway before their

destination for a similar reason. A month or two went
by, and I found myself loading and unloading at the
curb to that same casino again--the manager saw me
from the door, and a real-sour, disdainful look came
over his face: "you still drivin' for dem?"

It's hard enough to only get twenty-hours of work
per week with no benefits, but to have three-quarter
pay makes it even worse. Some drivers can make up
for low hourly pay by hogging more activity trips and
field trips--yes, I say "hogging" because then . . . the
new driver turn-over is tremendous year-after-year,
because there's no sense of reciprocity. What I'm talking about here is simple: let's say you have ten routes
and ten drivers, plus an extra regular driver who can
trouble-shoot or float from route to route where
needed, all averaging about twenty hours a week; then
a trip needs to be assigned: all the transportation director has to do is look at the next name on the rotation
and offer the trip to that regular driver, then that driver
has an option of passing that trip to the next driver on
the rotation--some drivers may pass every chance they
get for a trip, and some drivers will grab every chance,
but no one driver hogs all the gravy, and no one driver
is left with just crumbs off the table.

This subject is particularly sensitive for me, because
I have tightened my belt about as much as I can stand,
from the outside--driving a twenty-year-old mid-size
pickup, living on the cheapest land with the cheapest
housing, and I don't have any alimony payments or
child support. I get twenty-some hours on a good
week, and sometimes I'm lucky to get ten or twelve, . . .
while other drivers that are pickier about their assignments think it's unfair when they dip below forty
hours--they have new-car payments and big mortgage

payments. In these 2009-and-future hard economic times, everybody's got to give in, not just a few of us nice guys.

The old "good ole boy" network is making life unfair for a lot of people, and this "not what you know but who you know" nonsense has got to stop--it's going to do our planet in if we're not careful. We've got to correct this, or the human species is dumber than the rest of the Animal Kingdom. Go ahead and quote me on this: "The Human Race is the only species dumb enough to think it's smarter than the rest of the Animal Kingdom."

Some of the better drivers may not even care about the pay, and they do school-bus driving more as Volunteer Work, since they have kids in school or something, while the husband brings home the real bacon. I knew a preacher who took a regular route more as an atonement for some sin he'd committed in his younger years--he made me think of Nick Nolte in *Cannery Row*. But this generous attitude does not help the high percentage of drivers who need the pay.

The **Lack of Respect** For Good Drivers

It's important to address one big reason School-Bus Drivers have trouble gaining respect in far too many school districts around the country; it is: **mistakes made by too many drivers** themselves. I was fortunate to have a few of the best teachers in the country when I first started. Bear McKinney, just a regular route driver really--when he first checked me out, he made sure I knew how to really stop at a stop sign, so he didn't let me make any "Hollywood stops." Then, out on the open highway, he made sure I started looking down the road, like a half-mile out, to see the whole big picture--this is how you prevent a lot of potential trouble, or even avoid trouble already happening. (The best writers make sure they do this too, See the Big Picture.) Too many school-bus drivers drive their bus with their "car habits," barely seeing past the hood ornament, and they never got their much-needed "bus habits." Jack-rabbit starts-n-stops have no place with a school bus; when you pull away from a loading or unloading, it should be "at idle speed," as most manuals suggest--this is especially true around the younger children. It's not the big fiery spectacular crashes that get younger children; it's the slow pull-aways, even a measly 1/2-mph, when a child unexpectedly goes to retrieve a ball or some art-work too close to the bus or even Grandma's car. It's something I call the "Soccer Mom Syndrome," where the driver is in too much of a hurry, multi-tasking and running dozens of errands in the name of really getting the job done so they can move on to the funner parts of life. When I am finally loaded at a school, when I pull away from the curb, at idle speed, one of my pet-peeves is to see the school bus behind me crowding me and pulling away with me as if our two buses are connected with a tow-rope.

I had a charter-bus driver one time mad at me at a Texas truck-stop break in the middle of the night because he'd almost rear-ended me. It was a big military charter with about six or eight buses spaced each about five seconds apart. The way it works is this: the most senior driver with the newest bus goes in front, then the last bus is the newest company driver in the oldest bus--the one basic rule on a multi-bus trip is simple, "keep track of the bus behind you, so no one gets left behind." Now, cruise control is nice, and I use it when it makes sense, but I probably turn it off more than most drivers so that I can blend in with the circumstances a little better. If the bus in front of me that I'm following chooses to go through a 45-mph construction zone at 65-mph, that doesn't mean I have to. So the problem was, the guy behind me wasn't following me, he was following all the buses in front of me, which is wrong; and he was leaving his cruise control on too often. One little detail is, the buses in front of me were newer automatics, and the buses from mine rearward were still seven-speed sticks--so naturally, I would have a harder time keeping up, but the guy behind me was driving aggressively to make up for not having an automatic. This guy was older than me, and "used drive for Loretta Lynn," so I thought he should know better--"if you want to rear-end me, that's your business," I told him.

I've had a lot of OTR drivers mad at me because I "couldn't keep up." Well, I make no apologies, because I'm more courteous than they are: I turn my cruise control off in heavy traffic, and I share the road with the vehicles around me--some drivers won't turn that cruise control off for anything, or they won't let other vehicles have a piece of the road when they need it. It's like when you merge from two lanes down to one: you can either let the slower guy keep going, or you can hog the road in such a way with oncoming traffic that he has to careen off the road and come to a complete stop. A lot of these guys think they're part of the Blue Angels, but they're forgetting the Blue Angels don't have a bunch of ground traffic to contend with. I am of the "One-Bus/One-Driver" philosophy--that's why a lot of us become a professional driver, so we don't have bosses and fellow employees breathing down our neck. And I don't have a lot of patience for rude or aggressive driving. I like to think of myself as an Assertive Driver; I will accommodate the bad drivers to a point, but I don't want to give in so much as to invite or encourage their bad behavior.

But back to School-Bus Drivers. The way we drive around the general public has a lot to do with how much they respect us. If you drive a forty-foot bus like busy soccer mom in a mini-van, jumping curbs and cutting people off, seeing your driving as just another chore to get out of the way, that's not good advertising.

We've learned so much about school-bus driving over several decades, things have really gotten down to a science. It's a bus driver's job to get to know this science. When you see two good bus drivers doing the job right five states away from each other, chances are they are doing things much the same way--this school-bus science has some definite common denominators. For instance, there are right ways to design and drive school-bus routes (which we'll get to), and there are wrong ways: if a district or a driver has their own peculiar quirks, when the substitute driver shows up, no one will be on the same sheet of music, and this puts the little ones at risk. If you have one driver per each route for five years, and they each can do their route at break-neck speed with their eyes closed, suddenly when a new driver shows up for any of the routes, he's twenty minutes behind schedule every time he subs, and the whole community may think he doesn't have what it takes to do *anything* right. The pacing-n-rhythm and directions of a bus route need to be such that any other CDL-B-PS can come along and do it pretty much the same as the regular driver who's been doing it right all along. . . . Too many regular route drivers get too possessive of their routes: not only do they have their route-design quirks, but also they have put out an air that only the one driver can have control of the route--the kids won't obey a new driver, and the parents won't trust a new face, and on-n-on it goes . . . to scare off another new driver. One school district I subbed for was primarily routes driven by Moms, and most of these Moms were either related or good friends: every stop, you had to know the ridiculous idiosyncrasies: "honk twice from the corner," "give this kid about thirty-more seconds," "stop only if the curtain is half open"--for a sub, it was a dangerous nightmare. The regular "Mayberry-type" route drivers had all the kids and parents spoiled; and, when a driver came in from the outside finally trying to do things right, no one knew what to make of it. When you don't perform a school-bus route right or routinely--and I'm reminded of *Back To the Future's* Christopher Lloyd when I say this,-- . . . you can throw off the whole space-time continuum.

The next cause for lack of respect for school-bus drivers: **Mistakes made by the Administration.** The School Administration needs to support the drivers anyway they can and back good drivers in times of conflict. The link between the Highest Administration and the School-Bus Drivers . . . is the Transportation Director. Frankly, this ought to be someone with extensive school-bus-driving background; if the Transportation Director has never driven a bus before, he probably doesn't have the experience or the feel necessary for managing drivers or knowing their problems. If the school district is so small it can't afford all of what I'm suggesting, then whoever is in charge of transportation had better be consulting with the drivers to find out how things could be handled most smoothly. The Transportation Director should not be overworked: if he or she is more concerned about the air-conditioning in the auditorium . . . or the painting of the lines on the football field . . . or a clogged toilet in a mddle-school rest-room, important stuff, I'm sure, school-bus issues can too easily take a back seat--important decisions about school-bus and driver management . . . should not be an after-thought. In other words, whoever is the Conductor of the Orchestra . . . does not have to even know how to play all the instruments, but it sure helps (--I've often felt like that obscure guy in the back row . . . holding the cymbals, just waiting for the signal).

If the Transportation Director gets wind of drivers not driving as well as they should, he needs to take them aside to get them the necessary refresher training--it could be something as simple as "Slow down." It's always good to remind drivers: "Space Cushion." But there may not be much to worry about here if the drivers have been trained right in the first place. Some of my training happened before I even became a bus driver: pulling big ten-horse gooseneck trailers with dually pickups was good preparation, and ranch manager Bob McConaughy was a fine teacher.

Too many Administrations have a false notion that the school teachers and coaches are better than the bus drivers: the teachers' and administrators' jobs take more years of college and pay higher, so then they think there's nothing to bus driving, and they may think the drivers themselves aren't smart or don't have any ambition. Well, I am going to let everyone in on a little secret: **A big part of a school-bus driver's job is--are you sitting down?--. . . COM-MU-NI-CA-TION.** Just the way we handle the bus in and around other motorists is communication; the way we get along with the kids is communication; the way we deal with upset parents is communication; the way we serve the teachers and coaches on long trips is communication; and our relationship with the administration . . . is communication. . . . **But communication is a two-way street,** . . . and school-bus drivers have more two-way streets than all other professional drivers combined. I don't know how many times I've taken pride in doing this huge part of my job . . . only to be met with condescending . . . dumb looks. Hence this book.

Perhaps a few good drivers have trouble communicating with the administration and teachers and parents . . . because more than a few mediocre drivers give up trying. You report a few red-light violations, and they don't get followed-through-with by the authority above you, so why report any more? You try to deal with some kids' misbehavior, and it doesn't get properly dealt with from above, so why bother?

I had a transportation director one time, talking to me about some unhappy basketball coaches, tell me the old worn-out cliche about how "Respect is something you have to earn." Full of grey hair by now, I reminded him I'd spent the last twenty-five years trying to earn respect. I also reminded him, by virtue of my CDL license and its PS Endorsements, Respect is not something I should have to go out of my way to earn every time a new face steps on my bus--after all, **their safety is in the palm of my hands,** if not in my pocket. No, in the overall scheme of things, it makes sense to respect your bus driver, even if he is a strange "new guy," . . . perhaps even more than the shiny Badge of a Highway Patrolman, who could be corrupt . . . and doesn't necessarily have your safety in the palm of his hands.

Yep, RESPECT and COMMUNICATION--we can either do it the easy way . . . or the hard way. The book is the easiest way for me.

The deeper an administrator is in the system, the more insecure he may be, because he is not as free as say a bus-driver who can change states at a moment's notice--and this never gets noticed or talked about,--so they need to strut around more important every year, finagling things in their own favor, much like those highest in our U.S. Government. Tiny bus drivers can come and go easily: once you've got your CDL-B-PS and the other accoutrements, there's ten-thousand other school districts or bus companies or sand-n-gravel companies that could use you--this means freedom (and we'll address more why in a later chapter). Unfortunately, as a result, there's been a game of Musical Chairs going on among bus-drivers and truck drivers and job-openings for decades all over the country--you can change jobs all the time, but the next one usually ain't any better, and it could be worse. . . . So, when a good driver does his job right, it can often go overlooked by the administration--it's more often taken for granted, and they don't take responsibility for the high turn-over. **Most of the time, it's what doesn't happen on a bus route that matters: the kids that don't get run over, the accidents that are prevented or avoided, the kids that don't get left on a bus overnight, and so on--too much of this is unnoticed by the Administration, so the job is seen as unimportant,** especially compared to say police work or ski-patrol. But, mark my word, nowhere in the school system, counting teachers, coaches, administrators, janitors, maintenance, . . . is there more responsibility taken on for kids' safety than by the bus drivers--you can look it up. Doing a good job complete with communication . . . can even be misconstrued by the Administration--as they aren't used to a new sub driver standing his ground and asserting himself on important issues, and they could even ignorantly perceive it as insubordination.

When a bus driver gets that S-Endorsement for the School-Bus Stop Arm, they have a portable traffic signal under their jurisdiction. When there is a red-light violation by a motorist, the school-bus driver is obligated to radio in and report it. It's the Transportation Director's responsibility to follow through and get the report to the Law Enforcement Agencies involved--and that motorist should be issued a ticket and fined. When I worked for the Teton County School District in Jackson Hole, Wyoming, I had the route to a world-famous destination ski area, so I had more red-light violations than many routes combined. My boss understood that, and so he backed me every time. This was back in the mid- to late-1980s, and the initial fine was around $200; but, if a driver fought it and took it to court, where I had an obligation to be a witness, they had to pay close to $1000. Keep in mind, Bear McKinney taught me early on to get a natural feel for using the stop-arm, trying to time it so you don't make any cars stop unless you really have to. In a few other school districts I've worked in since then, any red-light violations I've reported have gone un-dealt-with, snubbed by the Transportation Director--it gives a flagrant signal that the driver doesn't matter, and the license doesn't matter, and even the kids' safety doesn't matter.

Then there's the matter of disciplining kids' bad

behavior on or around the bus. Generally, the policy in most school districts for bad behavior is this way: you give a couple of verbal warnings, and then you write the kid a ticket that makes it official he needs discipline, and the parents are notified by the Administration, and so on. It could be the kid is running up and down the aisle, or sticking his head out the window yelling at little old ladies, or throwing things at oncoming cars--there's a lot of ways to misbehave. The problem is, the paper ticket method sometimes takes too long, several days, when some consequences need to be felt by those involve sooner, in order to make the correlation; but it seems to be the best legal way nowadays; so, maybe three tickets, and the kid is off the bus for a week, putting the problem in the lap of the parents who will have to drive the kid to-n-from school themselves. Another problem is, sometimes the Administration gives a kid some kind of other punishment other than bus-related, like having them mop the cafeteria instead of revoking their bus privileges. Then another problem is, some of the regular route drivers don't ever write tickets, not even one in five school years; so then, when a substitute driver comes along and reports the bad behavior officially, it looks like it's never happened before--and it may even give the ignorant impression that the new driver is what brought out the bad behavior, therefore making the regular driver shine even more.

I don't know how many times I've subbed a route where the regular driver, the parents, and the administration, and the kids had things turned around backwards. I call it **"The Substitute Syndrome,"** just a total lack of respect for substitute bus drivers all the way around. But it's the Administration's responsibility to get everyone on the same sheet of music. I had a kid's grand-dad one time tell his grand-son, "You behave now! or you're gonna deal with me!"--but what I needed him to say first was, "You listen to your new bus driver now, and do what he says." It's the same with the Administration and the regular driver; they need to inform the kids the right way also. I don't know how many times I've had difficult kids try to tell me, "This isn't your bus, it belongs to Mrs So-n-So, so we don't have to listen to you!"--WRONG. When any driver is assigned to a bus, it's his baby, . . . but I stopped putting a "Tip Jar" on the school-bus dash a long time ago.

Keep in mind, a Substitute Bus Driver is not exactly the same as a substitute teacher. Substitute Teachers go through hell, I know, because I tried that for one school year, and that's a whole problem in itself. But a Substitute Teacher isn't expected to know everything of the subject matter and what-not like the regular teacher, so it's kind of a casual day for the kids, and the substitute teacher just tries to take roll-call and quell any riots. But a substitute bus driver has to know more than a regular route driver: he's got more routes to know, more buses, more stops, more kids, more sce- narios--the seasoned sub ought to be the highest paid driver. The young new substitute driver is at a total disadvantage, and we lose a high percentage of them after just a couple months of hell. I happen to be one of the few older seasoned drivers who's done a hefty amount of substituting--the kids and parents who don't know me find out real quick "this ain't my first rodeo"-- it wouldn't hurt my feelings any if they called me af- fectionately . . . "Dirty Gary."

Yet sometimes even an old seasoned substitute

may not know what all is going on with kids riding. I had a condescending teacher come on to a bus I was subbing one time . . . to assign seats for me. What she really should have done is taken this driver aside and explained the things that this driver did not know about--the sub driver definitely has a "Need to Know." Instead, she gave everyone the impression that the driver has no control.

I don't know how many times I've had Special Needs Aides give me a dumb look when I had a question about a given Special Needs passenger. If there is a health danger or a behavior issue with a certain student, the driver needs to know about it--even if he is a sub and a stranger, to boot!

Part of the problem is something subliminal or subconscious in the word "substitute" itself, that no one but yours truly has ever dug up or stopped to consider, : . . . **the word "sub" . . . subliminally gets linked up with the common prefix "sub-"** which means "lower, below, underneath," as in words like "subjugation, submission, subnormal, subordinate, subservient, substandard," and so on; so those three tiny letters "sub" . . . subtract from the true weight of the term "substitute driver." So the pay for a sub driver is often substandard even compared to the already-low pay of some regular drivers, barely enough to subsist on. I don't subscribe to this substantial subconscious attitude; and I submit . . . that we don't need a subcommittee to figure this out now that I've let the cat out of the bag. (Man, talk about subtleties and substance in fine writing. Maybe this book deserves a subtitle. And isn't is interesting? . . . that "sub" . . . spells "bus" backwards. Wow.)

Of course, there are more mistakes made by

passengers, parents, teachers, and coaches, in their perceptions of bus drivers, but these are greatly caused by the mistakes made by the Administration and some Drivers themselves. (We can deal with more of these isuues in later chapters.) One thing I loved about my idol Knowles Smith: whenever we had a problem, he would always talk to me and the other parties about it, and he always complimented me on my ability to communicate.

In all fairness, I have had some tremendous support over the years from some school administrators-- sometimes. I'll never forget subbing a route for a few weeks, a spoiled route where it got so bad the middle-school assistant principle came on my bus and gave about a five-minute speech addressing the kids in trouble. It was my new friend, the eloquent Tim Raban. I'll never for him asking permission to come on my bus beforehand. Then once on there, he laid it on real think, in the softest voice. He described how I was the captain of the ship, he emphasized how the Governor Herself--"The Governor Herself!--is not allowed on Mr Heins's bus . . . unless he grants her permission." Oh, how I wish I would have had a tape-recorder--I never dreamed that a school administrator could be more eloquent than yours truly.

The Pride of the Fleet

One relatively small school district I worked for bought a huge expensive late-model tour bus mainly for its varsity activity trips. The decision was made by the school board and influenced mostly by the football coaches, I believe; they didn't care what the Transportation Director had to say about how impractical it would be. All they cared about was having the big school logo rolling down the highway and parked in the rival team's parking lot, a couple-feet higher and five feet longer . . . overshadowing any peon school buses in the area. It was for team pride, school pride, crucial comfort of the players and coaches, and all that, so they could more easily win the state championship. Keep in mind now, this was one of the poorest counties in Arizona if not the whole country, but they claimed they "got a good deal"; yet this seven-year-old used bus cost, I believe, $175,000, and I' don't think that included the $60,000 paint job with the Redskin logo--they could have bought two or three brand-new school buses with that money . . . and made one of them the new trip bus, . . . or they could have given us drivers more pay.

What they didn't realize was that they had just hired a seasoned OTR driver who knew what a ridiculous decision it was. It was a 1998 Prevost, a forty-five-footer, twelve-feet tall, eight-and-a-half-feet wide, with very little ground clearance, bought in 2005. This behemoth was a bus that's a lot trickier to drive, because of its size and low ground clearance and excessive need for high technology. I knew something about the huge high-tech bus, because I had driven quite a few like it in my six-year OTR stint. When you have a bus like that, there's so much more to worry about; it's more like a space ship, and you can't feel it like a normal bus: going in and out of parking lots, you've got more things to concentrate on, like raising the rear-end or lifting the tag axle in tight places, remembering not to have the front-end lowered at the wrong time--I am reminded of that _Starship Trooper_ movie with Denise Richards first pulling out of that loading dock and making her driver-trainer nervous. Just forgetting where the door switch is can catch a driver with his underwear on the outside of his pants, even someone else's pants, especially if you're stuck on some rail-road tracks with a train coming. They figured out that only a handful of drivers should be authorized to drive this bus; and I noticed that, when some of the drivers wrote down the mileage in the paper work, they mistakenly put down 60,000, when in fact it was 600,000--a bus like that is designed to go a couple of million miles easily, like over a hundred thousand miles-a-year, like it had been doing before we bought it, . . . and they didn't know that was even possible, let-alone normal. A bus like that, to earn its keep, should be doing 500, 1000, or even 1500 miles-a-day, as it has the capacity to keep two or three full-time drivers in business; now, reserved for the more special occasions like varsity sports, it was relegated to doing less than a thousand miles-a-week, sitting for days without going anywhere. Meanwhile, they had an older trip bus that collected dust most of the time, because, as they claimed, "it over-heats too easily." A wiser purchase might have been two or three brand-new yellow school buses; or the older trip bus could have used some kind of mechanical work to keep it from over-heating. And maybe they just didn't understand that older trip bus: maybe the drivers were just driving it too fast on hot days, or trying to climb the steep grades in too high of a gear--there is a fair amount of finesse involved in handling buses.

The Prevost brand is about the most expensive brand in tour buses, starting at over $500,000 and going up over a million for the most famous celebrity country-music sangers. When I saw that bus, it told me where the Administration's priorities are--more with the bus than with the drivers. It's hard to clean both inside and out, there's no convenient place to frequently dump the rest-room; some of its routine maintenance takes experts who are two-hundred miles away, . . . and you've got to drive it often to stay sharp on your game. Whenever I drove "Big Red," I noticed a lot of civilians would stalk it on the highways or in the parking lots . . . to get a picture of it, indicating the driver is subservient to the bus.

In fact, part of the reason I got away from the OTR bus business when I did was due to the fact that the brand-new buses were getting stressfully too high-tech and uncomfortable for my tastes. My OTR stint was from 1996 to 2002, and, in those few short years, buses went from being easy pleasureable machines you could be a part of and feel . . . to being high-tech space-ships that could stress a driver out. When I started driving the big OTR buses in 1996, we had a fleet of two-hundred-fifty buses, and I could hop into any one of them and get it to fit me and know where everything was at; by 2001, the company had several makes and models, to where I couldn't get the seat and steering wheel just right on some models, and sometimes I could barely find the seat belt.

You get conditioned reflexes as a driver, which is something to consider, to minimize stress, which can maximize safety. One day, you're shifting a stick; the next day, you're in an automatic, but still reaching for the stick and clutch pedal; then, a week later, you're back in a stick-shift bus, and it's possible to forget to grab that stick and work that clutch pedal. When MCI (Motor Coach Incorporated) changed their seat-belt from the right side of the driver's seat to the left, about 1998, it put thousands of driver's off balance. Tired of most to the new bells and whistles, the erratic schedules, and always being away from home, <u>I decided</u> <u>slowing down to the fewer miles and fewer hours of</u> <u>basic school buses would be a nice way to get back</u> <u>down-to-earth.</u>

Fortunately, school-bus technology should stay relatively simple for years to come--a lot of it will be up to the administration and transport directors, what they choose to go with in their equipment purchases. I wish more drivers could be more awake and involved in bus design; but one gets the impression the engineers just change things for the sake of changing them . . . and then expect the drivers to love it because it' "NEW & IMPROVED." For instance, I would rather have a door handle that is strictly mechanical, like the old days, something I can feel for in the dark, instead of a push-button door where you can too-easily forget which button it is. You shouldn't have to get your trifocals on and start squinting just to open or close the bus door: there could be a bad guy you don't want on, I already mentioned being stuck on the train-tracks, and most bus drivers shouldn't have to consider it a luxury to be able to watch for pedestrians, especially school-bus drivers.

There is such a thing as too-simple technology though maybe. When I was employed with TNM&O Coaches, a subsidiary of Greyhound, occasionally they would use me to dead-head an empty Greyhound bus somewhere across the country. What I noticed right off the bat was most of the Greyhound buses, thousands of them, didn't have any steering-wheel adjustment, specifically no tilt adjustment--and you really need it if you want to keep your drivers from being miserable day-in-n-day-out. Any bus, I don't care how basic it is, should have the following adjustments available to the driver: the seat fore-aft, up-down, and the tilt of the back; the steering-wheel up-down and its tilt; and then the mirrors need to be easily adjustable--a lot of huge tour buses don't have large-enough mirrors. I noticed, at a state fair a few years ago, our U.S. Military Humvee didn't even have a fore-aft adjustment in the seat for drivers of all sizes--that's unconscionable. And some of the high-tech tour buses at the turn of the millenium wouldn't allow you to get the seat slid back far enough for an average-size driver. . . . And then we want to go to Mars and all that nonsense, like it's going to solve all our problems.

The Pride of the Fleet--I hope they keep the drivers in mind. Yes, The Pride could be a bus and not a driver, . . . but I hope it is a bus the drivers hold some affection for, . . . not a bus that pleases everyone but the driver. "No hoof, no bus."

Anatomy of a
School-Bus Route

It wouldn't hurt to shift gears now and talk about the actual job of school-bus driving. Some drivers new or old might learn something; and the civilian population can maybe start to appreciate what all it takes to run things smooth.

Pre-Trip Inspection

One of the most obvious parts of a school-bus driver's job is to get to his bus about twenty minutes before the route begins, to check the bus's working order, to make sure the bus is safe to drive and safe for the kids. I'm not going to give a full course in the inspection here; I just want to let the reader in on it. You get a routine where you can do it in the most efficient order--and a regular driver would get to know the idiosyncrasies of his main bus. If you are a substitute driver who may go days or weeks without seeing a bus, it's a good idea to make yourself a checklist on a little card. The pre-trip inspection, by law, needs to be performed at least once a day on buses used that day-- yet I worked for one school district that didn't want to pay the drivers for this measly fifteen minutes.

First, as you walk up to the bus, look it over **from a distance**, and try to see underneath--there might be something obvious right off the bat, like the bus leaning to one side because of a flat tire. Then you check **under the hood**: oil, coolant, power steering fluid, and maybe transmission fluid. It's often dark out before the sun comes up, and most drivers need a flashlight a good part of the school year. Visually check the belts and hoses, wiring and whatever else you might see-- you don't have to be a mechanic, but you can always get a mechanic or say no to a bus if something doesn't look right.

In the cab, you turn the key on just far enough to check the dash gauges and warning signals--diesel buses need you to take your time here anyhow. . . . Once you've fired the bus up, turn on the lights: head-lights and parking lights, clearance-n-marker lights, four-way flashers, eight-ways amber lights. . . . Your "eight-ways" are your four ambers and four reds, your portable traffic control signals, front and rear pairs of each, to control the motorists around you during pick-up and drop-off of the kids--this is one of the main reasons for your S-endorsement on your CDL.

It's a lot easier to check the rear turn signals, brake lights, and back-up lights if you have a helper outside the bus--I've been known to use a folding clip-board with a bubble mirror stuck on it. Use some common sense: if it's dark enough out, you can usually tell if your brake and back-up lights are working; and the four-way flashers won't work if your turn-signals aren't working.

At this point, your bus's door is shut, so the ambers are flashing, not the reds--you turn on the dome lights, get out of the driver's seat, and check for emergency equipment: reflective triangles, first-aid kit, fire extin-guisher. This starts your **walk down the aisle**: check the interior of the bus and security of the seats--make sure there's no transients on board. Of course, check the emergency exits: on the sides, in the roof, and the back door. Stick your head out the back door, and check those eight-way ambers, which are up high and alternate--don't confuse them with your four-way flashers, which are down low and flash together.

Now go back up front, grab you flashlight, open the main door, which will activate your reds, and get out for your **walk-around outside**. Start at the front: lights, especially your eight-way reds alternating, . . . mirrors, underneath. On the sides, you check your wheels for loose lug nuts or anything unusual, tires--use a night stick; and your brakes and suspension systems--you might use a hand mirror to see in tight places inside-around the wheels. Check the side compartments, and give a good look at the driver-train and exhaust system.

Probably after the left side and before the right side, you'll check the rear of the bus: lights, again especially your eight-way reds alternating, . . . tail-pipe, and underneath. You might catch something unusual here, like a rock stuck between the dual rear wheels.

Now you go **back in the saddle again**, to perform the air-brake check: pump down the brake pedal to lose the air--the low air-pressure warning signal should come on before it gets down to 60psi. As you keep pumping the air down with your foot, push in your yellow parking-brake knob in with your hand, and it should pop back out between 20 and 40psi. In other words, your spring-powered parking brake should take over whenever there is not enough air pressure for the air brakes. . . . Now, with the air pressure way down, watch your air-pressure gauges, and it should build back up from 85psi to 100psi in 45-seconds. As you mingle with your bus, you'll notice it spilling excess air from time to time, around 125psi-- this is the governor cut-in/cut-out business (so your bus doesn't build too much air). . . . One last thing: with the parking break now activated, yellow knob out, put the bus in gear, and see if the parking brake is strong enough to hold the bus still--the bus in gear shouldn't go anywhere and should kill the engine.

SB Pre-Trip Inspection

General Approach & Underneath

Under the Hood

   Oil, coolant, pow steering, tranny

   Belts, hoses, wires, more

In the Cab   --Gauges & Warnings

   Lights: head+park, clear+mark

     four-ways, <u>eight-ways</u> + stop arm

     turn signals, <u>brake lights</u>, back-ups***

   Wipers, fans + heaters

Walk Down the Aisle

   Triangles, f-aid kit, fire extinguisher

   Exits, seats, interior, <u>AMBERS</u>

Walk-Around Outside

   Front: lights+<u>REDS</u>, mirrors, underneath

   L & R: <u>STOP-ARM</u>, cmprtmnts, dr-train, exhst

    Wheels, brakes, suspension

   Rear: lights+<u>REDS</u>, tail-pipe, underneath

Back In the Saddle Again

   <u>**Air-Brakes**</u>

    Low AP Warning before 60psi

     P-brake knob --20-40psi, <u>P-brake hold</u>

    AP build-up: 85-100psi in 45sec

    Governor cut-in/cut-out

<u>**Time To Go**</u> --seat-belt, **steering play, brakes**

BackHomeAgain...CoolTurbo, <u>Check frKids</u>

   Engine Off, <u>AB-Leak Rate</u> (120psi)

    <2psi/min, then again <3psi/min

   Chock wheels, Drain air-brakes   #

When it's **time to go**, check the obvious: your seat-belt, steering play, and regular brakes. You should have a seat-belt cutter within reach, in case you have trouble undoing them in an emergency. If you didn't do it the first time you fired the bus up, now is a good time to check your windshield wipers, fans, and heaters and defrosters.

One of the ironic things about the pre-trip inspection is, sometimes it's the inspection itself that can wear out the mechanical parts involved. For instance, running your wiper blades on dry glass every time you turn around is harder on them than waiting for a little moisture. And killing the engine with a tug-o-war between the parking-brake and the transmission can't be all fun-n-games for all the mechanical parts concerned--it may not be a bad idea to perform it with a little more finesse without killing the engine every time. And cranking the large front wheels hard left or right parked on dry ground, to check steering components, may be what wears out those concerned components the most in the first place--this is why it's a good idea to use a hand mirror to look into those nooks-n-crannies (and it can be the same mirror you use to pluck your nose hairs with).

What I am trying to say here is, the best bus drivers aren't necessarily perfect, and maybe they don't even do every tiny thing by the book. But they're not neurotic either; and they don't have what Scott Peck would call a character disorder. **Good bus drivers just flat-out care:** they are not negative people--they don't spend all day shouting about how the world is coming to an end; they don't dwell on mistakes that could have cost dozens of people their lives--they move forward. Good bus drivers take responsibility for their job, even if they take a John Wayne Approach to some parts of it; good drivers are always monitoring their bus--if something goes bad during the trip, they try to be alert enough to notice it before it causes any trouble, but they don't panic at every little possibility. If you've got one little clearance light out in the middle of the back of the bus, and it's ten-below-zero out, and there are no spare buses, they're probably not going to string you up for continuing your run. . . . It may be that a little too much of this neurotic "What-If--?" business is ruining our country lately.

. . . Let's relax a minute. One of the most enjoyable things about school-bus driving can be the camaraderie with the boss and other drivers. Some of the longest routes tend to show up for work before 5-am, and these drivers may have it a little lonelier; but a lot of routes leave more like 6-am or later--these drivers can enjoy showing up about twenty-minutes to a half-hour before take-off time, spend ten- to fifteen-minutes doing the pre-trip inspection, and have ten- or fifteen-minutes to go inside in the driver's lounge, while the buses warm-up, where the boss always has a pot of coffee brewing. A lot of employers raise their hand and say, "No, we can't have drivers sitting around for ten or fifteen minutes every morning!" but I beg to differ, because this little extra time can come in handy more often than you think: besides boosting morale, it gives a driver a chance to get minor things fixed on a bus, or time to grab a spare bus if need-be, and it gives the drivers a chance to compare notes on kids' behavior or traffic problems or whatever. This scenario may be more common Up North, where half the year is pretty darn cold and snowy--therefore the people need to be warmer. A small restroom is well-appreciated by may drivers just before take-off time. If a school district doesn't have this little waiting area, like just outside the boss's office, with the smell of fresh coffee brewing in the air, the enthusiasm and morale and support won't be what it could be; then turnover will be greater, and training costs a lot higher, and safety won't be as high as it could be, because experience and routine will be lost in the shuffle--if you want to save money, look at the top-heavy costs of Administration. . . . Some school districts may think they've got this base already covered, this Driver Area already exists; but, if the driver's aren't using it, something is not quite right---the wrong location, too cold, not the right type of chairs, inappropriate lighting--consult Martha Stewart if you have to.

The Design of an **Actual School-Bus Route**

Before we get too far down the road, I just want to point out that school-bus routes can vary greatly, as there are a thousand factors that may shape a route: the size of the district, the size of the town, the layout of the town, where the kids are, where the traffic is, even the talent of the route designer, to name a few. So **shapes of routes vary**: some of the simpler routes are probably linear, like sending one bus in each direction; a small rural school might have a route that is more square or circular; and a limited number of buses with lots of nooks and crannies might make routes sort of star-shaped or tree-shaped with a lot of branches. Some routes, where families tend to have a lot of economic stability, don't change for years; while some routes might have to adapt monthly or even weekly as poor families play musical chairs with their slum-lords and constantly changing living quarters.. A Special-Needs Route might change fairly often, as passengers' needs change, needing a wheel-chair lift one week but not the next. ... At any rate, when designing a route or routes, the designer should lay out all the stops on a big map, get sort of a helicopter point of view of the layout. Then you might notice clusters of dots near each other, that might make an efficient route. ... I got into a school district one time, where the routes were all criss-crossed, and the kids were spoiled because several bus-driving moms had to haul their own kids whether it was on their way or not--it was a sub's nightmare, till someone came in from the outside and pointed out the dysfunctionality that had crept in over many years. ... Enough about that, let's get rolling.

First driving out of the bus barn or parking lot, regular drivers are usually very relaxed, being so familiar their bus and their routine. But, a substitute may have a little stress, because, while some drivers might be the same, every bus can be different. And, whereas regular-route drivers tend to gravitate toward getting a bus they like, a sub more-often has to take what comes whether they like it or not. Not every driver will have the same preferences.

I remember a Bus #3 I used to drive from time to time: it had a hair trigger for an accelerator pedal, and I always joked that the regular driver didn't have a regular mechanic working on it--"She takes her bus to a gun-smith," I joked. And, being #3, I called that regular female driver "Earnhardt" from time to time, affectionately, just because there's an ESPN movie that's been out for a few years now, *3*, about NASCAR Racing's legendary intimidator, Dale Earnhardt. Just another imaginary way for a driver to liven-up an otherwise mundane business. (Oh, by the way, I don't just have my Commercial Driver's License; I also have my

PWL, Poetic Writer's License.) . . . Interestingly, I had a ski family I gave a lot of ski lessons to back in the 1980s and '90s: Kip Laughlin was a Formula-One Race-Car Driver, and he said his nickname on the track was "The Yellow School Bus."

So, . . . on a typical bus route, the driver will drive out, say, ten or twenty miles empty, turn around at the farthest point, and then head into town, picking up kids along the way. It's a good idea to have like a five-minute buffer time at the turn-around or starting point--the longer the route, the more this is true, and the more minutes there should be. Some routes don't have this lag time designed into them, because the district may be too stingy or someone didn't know any better, and it puts a driver at a disadvantage right from the start, especially a substitute, with no room for error. The same is true for lag time between runs: you might pick up your middle-schoolers and high-schoolers on one run . . . and then make a second run for the elementary kids--there should be a lag time between the runs, so, if you're late getting the first run done, you don't have to be late starting the second run. Some of this can be tricky, I know, because of all the factors involved; but the Administration needs to understand the bus **Schedules-n-Timing** need to be relaxed and easy and routine, so that a substitute can perform it pretty much the same as the regular driver. In fact, if you take home the elementary and kindergarten kids before the middle-school and high-school, you should have time to check for the hidden little ones inadvertently still on the bus before you do the rowdy older-kids run.

If a bus route is timed right, you can hit every stop about the same exact minute every day. It's common for a driver to have a small clock stuck to the dash-board, or a sub might have to lay down his own watch; this time-piece should be set to the exact time, just like a cell-phone or your satellite TV--then theirs no question about what time the bus comes by. The bus should go the speed limit, or just a bit under, with no jack-rabbit starts or stops--every time you pull away from a stop, you're supposed to be checking those pedestrian mirrors, . . . and it's supposed to be "at idle-speed." Drivers who don't pull away from stops slowly "at idle-speed" are lucky they're not running over someone--safety with them is more of an accident.

Now we approach the most dangerous part of school-bus driving, loading and unloading. According to a fine government publication, *Head Start Driver & Monitor Training Manual*, when talking about pre-schoolers, kindergarteners, and elementary-age kids, "The most common way children are killed, is by being run over by their own bus." Then, "The second most common cause of a bus fatality is when a child is struck by a passing motorist. The younger the children, the greater the risk."

Sometimes young children and preschoolers and toddlers are taught to see school-buses in too festive of a light--there were times when I felt like a famous rock star,--and that can be dangerous for the little ones, even the family dog. And then kids get the wrong impression that they are immune to danger. . . . One time, while dropping off a kid at some low-income government housing, I noticed a young couple holding hands with a 2-year-old and walking toward the bus, sort of celebrating its arrival; . . . but, when they got within ten-feet of my stopped bus, they let go of the kid's hands, almost as if they were waiting to see would might transpire. --I got real suspicious real quick and tersely told them to get that child away from the bus.

Dirty Harry and them might like to talk about the "Stopping Power" of a .44-magnum revolver; but I have something more powerful: the **'Stopping Power' of a 'Loaded' School Bus.**" I've run this original expression by some of my colleagues, but they didn't seem too impressed by it, as they weren't really paying attention: they thought I was referring to the braking power of the bus--No! I'm referring to the Stop-Arm and Eight-Way Flashers, which are just as powerful as any other traffic signal, hopefully more. It's one of those creative metaphors or ambiguities or mouble deanings I'm famous for. So I'll say it again, and really listen: the **'Stopping Power' . . . of a 'Loaded' School Bus.** There's nothing worse than writing great stuff . . . that goes over your friends' heads.

. . . The kids should be out at their stop a few minutes before the bus arrives, especially if the driver is so precise from day-to-day--the driver should not have to toot the horn . . . or wait out on the road, holding up traffic for a late kid. You activate the amber lights between 500- and 100-feet before a stop, sort of depending on how fast you're going--these alternating amber lights are synonymous with the yellow light at an intersection, . . . and they mean "slow down, get ready to stop," not "speed-up, maybe you can beat the reds!" . . . So, when you come to a complete stop, in your lane of traffic, put the bus in neutral and set the parking brake; when you open the door, this cancels the ambers and activates the alternating reds and stop-arm--these are synonymous with a red light at an intersection. . . . I say "Stopping Power" because, even if an ambulance or fire truck were to show up while you're in the middle of this process, if your reds are already activated, they are required to stop for the school bus-- you can't be changing horses in the middle of the stream when it comes to the safety of school children. A law-enforcement vehicle--I'd have to see the situation, because they might be chasing a kidnapper or child-molester or something, but they are always the first to stop if they are not "in hot pursuit." Finally, when you close the door, this deactivates the red lights--and now you don't want to linger too long, because it would be real easy to get rear-ended with your traffic signal turned off.

The basic <u>Rules for the kids Loading</u> should be simple: (1) Be at your bus-stop a few minutes early; (2) Stay well off the road, with no fooling around; and (3) Board the bus quietly when it is safe to do so. . . . Basic <u>Rules for Unloading</u> should show common sense as well: (1) Be ready to exit when the bus comes to your stop; (2) Be careful unloading, watching for traffic, getting away from the bus and off the road quickly; and (3) Never run back to the bus to pick up something. On my first bus route, in Jackson Hole, I had to watch out for bicyclists even more than the cars sometimes, since they would come from behind and pass on the right shoulder, right where they could clobber and unsuspecting kid--I didn't have much sympathy for ignorant bicyclists, seeing as how I rode a bike myself . . . Older kids may not be in as much danger as the younger ones, but they need to set a good example for the younger ones. Of course, the younger the kids, the more they need an adult accompanying them to and from the bus stop. And how desolate a stop is out in the country can be another factor even for the oldest kids--you wouldn't want to drop them off with a ten-mile walk down a ranch road.

An important part of having that S-Endorsement on the CDL is knowing how to use that traffic signal "in the route place at the route time and under the route circumstances." I've had pre-school teachers assume I could whip it out any old time and for as long as the teacher wants, sitting in the middle of a busy street with toddlers using the bus as a set of monkey bars, while the teacher and parent discuss the upcoming Halloween Party--WRONG. This isn't like Kim Darby in True Grit, drawing Lawyer Daggitt every time she feels like it--"She draws him like a gun!" as Glenn Campbell points out. If you use the stop-arm willy-nilly, or time it so you make more cars stop than necessary, and take too long every time you use it, you're just irritating the other motorists to the point where they won't want to obey it. The use of the Stop-Arm is for planned routine stops mainly, although I did see a guy use it for a bunch of mule-deer crossing the highway at dawn one morning, and no one seemed to complain.

What I've noticed over the years, driving more scenarios than most other drivers: a high percentage of the general public honestly does not know what a school-bus's amber-n-red eight-ways are all about--and night-time is really no excuse. I've had cars in front of me on the highway pull over thinking I was the Highway Patrol or an Ambulance. I've had people who ran my reds testify in court that they though I was a snow-plow--like it's a good idea to barrel blindly around one of those. And I've had countless over-cautious people stop, on quiet roads and even on the highway, when I just had my four-way hazards flashing, which are standard on every car, . . . even when I was totally parked off the road--this will confuse or irritate the motorists behind them. The general public's ignorance is not entirely their own doing: they learn from the overall lack of respect from the administration on down, and they learn weird things from actual drivers that don't have a full grasp of their responsibilities and procedures.

So, no matter how well a driver uses the stop-arm and red-lights, children and parents must understand that other cars and trucks might not stop for them. More than a few times, I've had to use my Air-Horn to wake people up: first, you want to wake up the pedestrians involved when there's a danger; second, the air-horn wakes up the motorist not paying attention; and third, the air-horn blaring drums up witnesses both inside and outside the bus in case you need them. Yeah, the air-horn will scare the crap out of people, but it should, especially if it saves their life--and one good blast well-timed, may break them of the dangerous habit of being complacent the rest of their life. Even high-schoolers have become more vulnerable in recent years, with their lack of discretion using cell-phones or stereo ear-plugs during unloading--a driver really needs to crack down on that.

As I mentioned earlier, I've probably had more red-light violators than the average bus driver, because of the contributing factors on some of the routes I've driven. One time, and I felt for this guy a little bit, I had a guy run the stop-arm, slowly but surely, because my bus had the same number "23" as a parked bus in his neighbor's alley way--"I didn't think that bus was supposed to be in service," he said. A more flagrant violation: I had a young man flip me off and not even slow down as he ran the stop arm at 55mph; when we went to court, because he wanted to fight it, his explanation was "it was my friend's pick-up, and I was late for work." He lost close to $1000 on that one more than twenty years ago, but I probably lost ten times that much, since his girl-friend was the ski-school secretary where I was a ski teacher every day--she kept me from getting a lot of private-lesson assignments for a few years running. . . . That's okay: this book will help make up for it; it can't be too much longer before we meek inherit the earth.

Since then, I've had some teachers and other school employees make some pretty silly moves around the buses I've driven--and I sort of keep learning to keep my mouth shut. Another reason to get this book done . . . and make millions.

If they ever do make a comedy about school buses, I'd like to see one barreling down the highway at full speed with the stop-arm out, so that theoretically every car he meets "runs the stop sign"--even show a car driving backwards at 65mph in order to "not run the stop-arm." I could talk all day about red-light violations, . . . just like old Bob Graham, the safety director at TNM&O Coaches, could spend all day talking about "stale green lights"--we're passionate about it.

How Regular Drivers can Make it Easy for Subs

When regular drivers have their designated routes, things get pretty routine for them real quick--they might do a dry run a couple of days before school starts and have a pretty good go of it the first day of school. But, when a Substitute gets in their bus, he needs something more to go on than conditioned reflex or memorization; of course, riding the route and taking notes goes a long way, but that doesn't mean it's memorized, especially if a sub has ten routes to know. So most school-bus routes need a list of directions, at any driver's disposal, for remembering things on a spur of the moment. It may not be enough to have a list of the exact stops; if you don't know where to turn, the stops can become pretty meaningless--it can take a few minutes to look up one address, and then you still have to figure out how to get there. One rule of thumb, as long a s sub knows where to turn, then all he has to do is keep watching for kids: if theirs a kid there, it's a good-bet it's a stop; if there's a stop with no kids, well, then the kids are late and they missed their bus--it's not a subs job to go looking for late kids, especially when they don't know if there's even anyone to look for anyhow.

So the first main list on the bus should be the **Route Directions**, with times listed by the turns, and use bold print for main landmarks. I must say, being a writer, I'd have to say most people don't know how to give simple directions. You could be standing on the West Coast, within walking distance, asking people where the Pacific Ocean is, and they wouldn't know how to just point a finger to the west; some would have you driving east on a one-way street looking for two or three key turns before they realize you're on foot. But, okay, with a school-bus route, you need more details, but, to me, it's simple: a list of turns and roads is the easiest way to put it, not an elaborate bunch of paragraphs, just left or right, onto which road, and the direction one would be going as a result--the landmarks or **destination points** in bold print could enable a driver to ignore some of the more-detailed directions, but underline anything key. Take a look at this sample bus route, and it could be printed on a small card that the driver can hold easily in one hand while driving, the AM Route on one side and the PM Route on the other: . . . --See what I mean? Any unique parenthetical comments are off to the side, landmarks, and so on.

SB Route Directions

AM Rt#25	PM Rt#25
PreTrip **6:15am**	Punch-In **2:40pm**
BB 6:37 leave	**BB 2:50 leave**
LN 13W	**MS 3:05**
LW Clvlnd	**HS 3:10**
RW US-180 . . .	**Elem** (call)
CO-5152 7:00	W Clvlnd . . .
R SodFarm (M, Tu, F), Smiths (W, Th)	R 13W, L 17N (Donna's) arnd blk,
SE US-180A 7:15	R 13W
CO-5270 mailboxes, U-turn	RW Clvlnd . . .
NW US-180A, RE US-180	RW US-180 . . .
LE Clvlnd	CO-5152
LN 13W. . .	Smiths, T-arnd
LW 17N (Donna's) arnd blk	SE US-180A
RS 13W . . .	CO-5270 mailboxes, U-turn
LE Clvlnd, RS 4W	**PT-Inspect**
MS 7:42	NW US-180A, RE US-180
RW 7S (Chavez)	LE Clvlnd . . .
HS 7:50	RS 13W
Elem 8:00 **PT-Inspect**	**BB 4:40**
BB 8:15	###
#	

As far as the stops are concerned, the kids should be out there waiting, and they should be easy to spot by the driver from several seconds away. The times on the morning pick-up route need to be precise, and the afternoon departure times should stay precise, but the drop-off times don't need to be listed, though they'll stay about the same everyday without a driver even trying. Notice that L and R alone won' cut it, you really need N, S, E, W--all it takes is one wrong turn or one small question in a sub's mind, and L means R, and R means L, . . . or does it?

Now the Question arises about a **Roll Sheet** for who's riding the bus that day. This can be a separate sheet of letter-size paper on a convenient clip-board: this would be strictly the order of **the stops**, either by address or by an obvious landmark as each heading, and the time, . . . with a **list of the kids' names under each stop** on the left . . . and the **M-T-W-T-F AM/PM columns** favoring the right--if a sub driver picks up three kids he's doesn't know from Adam . . . at a stop with three names, chances are good that the kids' real names will match the names on the list. Also, when loading a bus at school, to take everyone home, the kid can inform the driver of which stop . . . and then give their name--that way, a driver can find a smaller list to make sense of. This Roll Sheet broken down by stops should be on one-page-per-run, not two or three pages, because there's nothing worse than a driver flipping pages while loading or unloading--with computers of the last umpteen years, all you have to do is make the margins small enough and the font sizes small enough. As a sub driver, I often enlist the help of a well-be-haved student or two to do the roll sheet--some of them are delighted that you would need their help. With elementary kids, about all you can get away with is asking a couple of more mature ones simple yes-r-no questions about everyone else's names--it's tricky ask-ing each kid for their actual name, as they can be slow and inaudible and impossible to understand in the heat of battle. Because of the more delicate needs of ele-mentary children and kindergarteners, they often get

Rt #9 Roll Sheet-- **Week of** _____

7:00 Stop Address Here	M	-	T	-	W	-	T	-	F	-
Kid Name										
Kid Name										
Kid Name										
Kid Name										
Number Riders										
7:05 Stop Address Here	M	-	T	-	W	-	T	-	F	-
Kid Name										
Kid Name										
Number Riders										
7:12 Stop Address Here	M	-	T	-	W	-	T	-	F	-
Kid Name										
Kid Name										
Kid Name										
Number Riders										
7:17 Stop Address Here	M	-	T	-	W	-	T	-	F	-
Kid Name										
Kid Name										
Kid Name										
Kid Name										
Kid Name										
Number Riders										
7:24 Stop Address Here	M	-	T	-	W	-	T	-	F	-
Kid Name										
Kid Name										
Kid Name										
Number Riders										
Grand Total Riders										

their own route, so hence their own list, which is smart of the school district, but sometimes they do ride with middle-schoolers and high-schoolers.

. . . One more thing: these one-page clerical records need to be done in fonts that are easy to read and not

IN ALL CAPITAL LETTERS, WHICH ARE EX-
TREMELY HARD TO MAKE SENSE OF FOR A SUB
WHO DOESN'T KNOW THE KIDS OR HAVE EVE-
RYTHING ABOUT A ROUTE MEMORIZED. You
shouldn't have to scan the whole list and be flipping
pages, and one of the dumbest things is to have two
more little names on a second page. I've seen lists of
like sixty names, in no particular order, on two or three
pages, and in all caps--this is impossible for a sub to
make sense of in the heat of battle, and you can't be in-
undated with a bunch of inefficient clerical work while
driving a bus with a bunch of loading or unloading in
traffic. As a sub, sometimes all you can do is the best
you can with what you have to work with; **just getting
the right number of riders at a given pick-up or drop-
off is a good start**--and don't feel guilty about putting a
clip-board on the back-burner if you really need to
concentrate on the driving.

So, anyway, the route directions are absolutely
needed, and a conscientious sub can do some of this
himself, as I have; but the Roll Sheet is maybe more
optional on a bus route--obviously it becomes more
necessary in the event of an accident, but it is not a sub-
driver's baby. It's interesting: whereas a regular driver
doesn't need Route Directions, a sub driver really does;
then, whereas a regular driver can make sense of a Roll
Sheet, the sub driver may not want to be bothered with
it unless it's absolutely necessary. Remember: school-
bus routes don't take all day, so the last thing you need
as a sub is an extra half-hour of clerical work in the
middle of a one-our bus run--and then a boss or parents or school cafeteria workers wondering what took
you so long. The younger the kids, the more difficult it
is to ask them their name and get an audible answer--

you can spend all day and never get the list right if you don't know the kids. . . . So, it's better to treat a lot of bus routes like the starting of a horse race, especially taking them home: get an accurate count, and then get the unloading underway before problems have time to manufacture themselves--before you know it, nine kids got off here, seven got off there, and the bus suddenly feels manageable again. Heaven forbid an innocent school-kid would turn up missing--this is one reason sub drivers need so much support. Remember, the kids know their routine, the parents know the routine, the teachers will call you on the radio if you missed one at the school, other regular drivers might know an idiosyncrasy they can share with you--you can't be a very confident substitute driver if you carry the whole weight of the world on your shoulders, wandering through life like a neurotic Robin Williams in *The Best of Times.*

Post-Trip Inspections

When you get done with a school-bus run, morning or afternoon, or anytime, you're supposed to check your bus for kids that might inadvertently still be on the bus--it's the Law. This **Prevention of Stowaway Kids** is one of the most important parts of a school-bus driver's job--you can go to jail for not performing this duty. But, sadly, there's always a percentage of school-bus drivers who shrug-off this chore--again, with them, safety is an accident. Even here in 2009, we still hear about kids being left on school buses overnight, or even over the weekend--the day-time leave-ons are probably more easily kept hush-hush, but these can be just as dangerous. We need to understand why this is so dangerous: the younger the kid, the quicker they can die, from excessive cold, excessive heat, no water; or they could wander off into the abyss. Handicapped or Special Needs passengers are more at risk also.

You'd be surprised how easy it would be to forget or not even know you have someone still on the bus-- every time it happens, the lame excuses pour out. Since school-bus driving has been gotten down to a science over the decades, it's wise to remember we have most policies for a reason: to avoid making the same mistakes over and over again. We humans can do it, we don't need a computer to do it for us; but we have to have a plan and stick with it.

Remember, whereas the pre-trip inspection is only required once a day when you start, **this post-trip inspection for kids is done after every run**, not just at the end of the day--a small child can die just as quick at 12-noon on a hot day as 12-midnight. And, for the record, it's better to check right there at your last drop-off point . . . than driving back to the bus-barn first. Your last drop-off point could be fifty miles out of town, or it might be at the curb at the elementary school. When I've dropped off at an elementary school, I pull up a few yards out of the way to let the rest of the buses pull in and drop-off: I've noticed, when they get done dropping off, almost all of them make a bee-line for the bus-barn on the other side of town, zipping right around me and giving me a look like "Why are you parked there?"--"Well, I'm just doing my job, the same way you're supposed to." . . . One thing about doing the post-trip inspection after every run: you need time between runs to allow for this; I've seen bus runs on so tight a schedule they don't allow for the measly two or three minutes you need. Maybe it seems more important for me to perform this chore more than other drivers for the following reason: when you're as smooth a driver as I am, it's all too easy to put your passengers to sleep.

. . . Now, back at the barn, we're not quite done yet. You should idle the engine a couple more minutes to let it cool down in a friendly manner, especially if there is a turbo-charger like a lot of buses have nowadays. And, related to your pre-trip inspection, you should monitor your Air-Brakes Leak Rate: the Air Pressure is around 120psi when you turn the bus off; and, as the bus goes beddy-by, it will start to lose air pressure, but it should not drop 2psi the first minute, . . . and not drop 3psi more during the second minute. I know this can sound complicated, but it's not that bad, it just takes a little time. When you see a bus zip in to the bus barn, and the driver is out in less than five seconds, you can tell they didn't do any of this. Anyway, now we are done, . . . unless you want to sweep the bus or check for stowaways one more time.

Whenever I park a bus, I try to get it to "settle in" where it won't roll away even if the parking brake is off or the wheels aren't chocked. It's nice if your parking spot is level and has little depressions in the gravel where the wheels can settle in. One dangerous thing about big buses that few people ever consider: you could have the parking brake on, with the yellow knob pulled out--well, someone, whether it be a passenger or the driver, could bump that knob accidentally, and then you've got 30,000-pounds-or-more of bus rolling. Chocking the wheels can be a chore, but you do it when you have to.

Oh! one more thing: once you are really done and outside the bus, you might need to drain the air-brake lines of any moisture. In wet or wintry weather, moisture can get in the air lines, from condensation and what-not, and make it so you won't have the air pressure you need next time you fire up the bus. Now's the time to do it, when the bus is warm in the middle of the day or before the cold of night sets in. A lot of drivers get caught off guard one cold morning, when the moisture has settled and frozen in the lower parts of the air line, so they can't get any air pressure built up. It's fairly simple, but remembering to do it is the hard part: older buses had a little valve or two you would turn open with your fingers, then buses had spring-type valves you could nudge with a broom handle, and the easiest more-modern setup is a cable you can reach for and pull just like the air horn has. It's something you want to tinker with on a warm sunny day, so you don't end up crawling under the bus with a flashlight in the frozen mud looking for these valves--there are usually two, but it could vary. Just open the valve to squirt some air out, and you'll see the moisture if there is any--it's powerful enough to spray a crater into the gravel, so you wouldn't want to clean your glasses with it. Some buses are more susceptible than others, just like some drivers.

Speaking of sweeping or cleaning the bus, it depends some on the route, some on the driver, and some on the Transportation Director. Being a substitute driver on many many different routes, I've seen the full gamut: some regular drivers keep their bus spotless, . . . and others keep theirs down-right dirty; but, here again, we don't always know the whole reason why buses may be kept clean or are allowed to go dirty. When I started with Knowles Smith in the mid-1980s, his policy was for drivers to sweep their bus when it needed it, which could be one to five times a week, . . .

and give it a thorough cleaning inside once a month; the outside cleaning was left to the two mechanics as needed--it gave them something to do when they didn't have too much mechanical stuff going on. Usually a good bus-cleaning happens right after a morning run: it could take an hour, and a driver needs to know he'll be compensated for it--not being paid to clean a bus could be the only reason it's allowed to go dirty.

For what it's worth, when it comes to cold-morning pre-trip inspections, hot-afternoon parkings, mid morning cleanings and so on, I like my bus barns or garages or sheds to face the best way to keep the buses and drivers and mechanics comfortable throughout the day. In the cold north, I loved it when the buses had a southern exposure all day long. In the not-so-cold southwest, I liked it best with eastern sun to warm you up in the morning, but shade for the western sun to keep you cool during the hottest part of the day. Planning or observing this kind of thing makes a huge difference, in my book, especially if you find yourself in that bus-barn environment five days-a-week for many school years. In Jackson Hole, we had some in-door parking because of the extreme cold: I always liked it when Knowles would call me from his roving pick-up, Unit E, to tell me to park in Bay 6--"Back to Basics," I thought, "and Unity"--those are good ideas always.

Reflecting on Kids' Behavior

Unlike other driving jobs, school-bus drivers are expected to know what's going on behind them--the rear-view mirror is the largest of any commercial vehicle, and what the kids are doing is a big part of the driver's business. When I've been unsupported by parents or transportation directors for trying to keep the kids under control, I've joked that we need to sit with the driver's seat turned-around facing the kids, then we can put up the mirrors to see where we're going. Because of a driver's responsibility of not only safe driving . . . but also keeping some kind of order on the bus, . . . the big broad inside overhead rear-view mirror . . . can be described accurately as . . . the bus's most dangerous piece of equipment--it takes a knack for knowing when to glance at it . . . and when to ignore it. . . . They say that the best school-bus drivers . . . "have eyes in the back of their head"; but, throughout this book, you'll notice . . . it helps to have "a head in the back of your eyes."

The <u>Riding Rules</u> of a school-bus need to be kept simple: (1) No hazardous items allowed on the bus; (2) Remain seated, facing forward, keeping the aisle clear and keeping the windows clear; (3) and Talk quietly, with no obscene language, but let the driver know if you need help. The ground rule before any others is, of course, the driver is in charge of anything that happens on or around the bus. . . . A school-bus is not a democracy, where majority rules, but a dictatorship, where one person rules, the adult driver in charge--not a mean dictatorship like Saddam Hussein's, mind you, but a dictatorship nonetheless; even if it were a democracy, the driver in charge is the only one of voting age anyhow. . . . I second the motion. All those in favor, . . . say "I." . . . "I." . . . All those opposed, . . . say "Neigh." . . . The "I's" have it. . . . I might have to start carrying a gavel on my dashboard . . . and maybe start wearing a fancy gown like a judge. . . . But, here again, I've seen Bus Riding Rules with lists twelve items long, which means they are too complificated and redundant--it ends up sounding like a big court case where everyone's got to hire lawyers to get along. Just keep it simple; and, in the heat of battle, the driver has the final ruling. Often-times, you can confiscate contraband for a short while without making a federal case out of it. Sometimes you've got to show some compassion for the kid or a piece of birthday cake or some show-n-tell item, letting a frog or toad live, for instance, instead of releasing it on a city street.

It takes a lot of imagination to get along with the kids--they don't like a gestapo, except for the ones on *Hogan's Heroes*. The more you can divert their attention sometimes, the less trouble you'll have, kind of like Danny Glover does in *Places In the Heart*. I've given a lot of kids "Homework Assignments" over the years, just for fun, telling them they'll get "extra credit." The more time you spend hauling the same kids, the easier they tend to obey you; but it can be extremely rough if you only see some loads once or twice a year-- as a sub has to try to gauge how strict or lenient each regular driver is. The first time kids see a sub is the most likely time they will try to test you--**the kids can be tricky**--and you can bet your life on it, regardless of what their parents will tell you.

The first day I ever drove a bus, there were hard copper pennies being hurled periodically from the back of the bus--that's as bad as an air-rifle. Recently, I caught a high-school senior throwing something hard out the window at an oncoming SUV at highway speed, which is the equivalent of a 130mph projectile!-- I seen him getting ready to do the dirty deed, and he didn't know I was ready. . . . One time, in town at a stop-light, I had a driver of a beer truck jump out of his rig in the middle of the busy street and start pounding on my bus door--he was after one of my high-schoolers in the back who had thrown something out the bus window at him in traffic. The list goes on. . . .

When there is misbehavior on a school-bus, it's important to deal with it early on, so you don't let the kids get spoiled with bad habits. The worst behavior is probably that way because they get away with too much at home . . . or maybe in school . . . or with other bus drivers. It's important to be fair with all ages; but, if you get it wrong with younger ones, you're liable to be causing more damage. This is why, the younger and bigger your load, you don't want to dawdle so long that you constantly have issues arise--with little ones, it's too easy to get things twisted around as to who's guilty or who's innocent. I had one little boy get in trouble one time for punching a little girl; but, a few days later, I realized three or four little girls might have been egging him on for several day beforehand--it's harder to sort it all out on a bus, compared to what teachers and parents can observe on the playgrounds and in the classrooms.

One time, early in my career, I had an eighth-grade boy who was cussing a little too much in his normal conversation with his buddies. I even had fellow female driver JoAnn riding with me that day, sort of seeing how I was doing. A short time later, as we were parked in a big lot unloading several kids, I took him aside for some friendly guidance. I suspected he had learned his new words from his own Dad, so I showed some compassion, saying, "Just don't do it in front of women and children." He got a kick out of the fact that I treated him like a responsible young man--I think he felt like a good guy in a John Wayne western,--and I never heard any more cussing out of him. JoAnn, who had more experience than me, could have handled it, but I think she wanted to see how I would handle it, . . . and she got a kick out of it too.

It's important to reward the good behavior. One of the main guidelines I try to remember while getting along with kids is from the great Colt Breaker Ray Hunt, something like this: "Notice the smallest change and the slightest try, and reward it"--what's "better" behavior for one kid . . . might not be exactly "better" behavior for another kid. Like great horse trainers who don't very often use grain to bribe their horses with, I don't quite agree with handing out candy to little kids, like many regular drivers do, for two more reasons: the parents might not want it, and it can be distracting during unloading. A kind word well-timed goes a long way. With older kids with longer rides, if the bus has a tape or CD player, I might put on some soothing Ray Price or Al Green as a reward, just like I do for horses back at the corral--it might be some kids' only chance to hear such fine music. If they misbehave, I threaten to sing for them, in my own voice. I often thought about offering a prize for "My Millionth Passenger," bit I never got around to it (--maybe "My Millionth Reader" will get something).

. . . Of course, don't forget: **the kids can also be pretty-darn cute and innocent sometimes**. They love to show you their art-work . . . or their science project, and they like it even more when you first show the interest. They like a bus driver who has a sense of humor. Though I never got around to it, I always dreamed of showing up on Halloween either dressed like a stage-coach driver (complete with chewing tobacco and a plastic double-barrel shot-gun) . . . or a NASCAR race-car driver (complete with the crash helmet and fire-proof suit). Anything you can do to keep the kids knowing you're on their side, the better. Or you just need to be able to divert their attention from time to time.

One time, subbing a route years ago, I had a 15-year-old mentally-retarded girl in the front of the bus who couldn't keep her hands to herself--it was hard on the little kids up front, and then they would retaliate. In fairly short order, I realized all I had to do was divert the older girl's attention: "Which way now? Which way now? Do I turn here? Or do I turn at the next one?" I was able to keep her busy the whole route for a number of days in a row: "Not yet," she would guide me, "Go straight, go straight, . . . now turn!" and she was so glad to help.

One time, I had a bus-load of elementary kids where we had to pull over and wait for a rendezvous with another bus. I noticed I was about seven minutes early, and the kids were already pretty rambunctious. I didn't know what I was going to do to keep them quieted down. Then I came up with a plan: I stood up and got their attention . . . and asked them if they wanted to play musical chairs. Suddenly they were all ears--they had never heard of being allowed to play something as wild as musical chairs on a bus before; so now I told them that, "If we do this, we have to follow some rules." So I set out to explaining all the rules to them, which I could use up a few minutes doing. In the middle of my rules explanations, one of the older more savvy second graders pointed his finger at me and said, "I know what you're doing." Pretty soon, the other bus showed up around the bend, . . . and then I announced we had to post-pone our little game. Whew!

One time, about early November, I was subbing a

route on South 19th Avenue, south of Bozeman, with a bunch of elementary kids. It was a straight black-top with a fresh new layer of the slickest ice--you couldn't even stand up on it. My bus was headed up the gentle grade south, which is a little easier than coming down. Well, there was a full-size Ford pick-up coming down that gentle grade toward us. Looking way out like I'd been taught, I saw him coming more than a half-mile away. Still more than a quarter-mile away, he started fish-tailing: . . . left, . . . right, . . . left, . . . right, ... It was slow and beautiful, like a pendulum, and so far away--I wasn't too worried because I figured he'd be safely into the soft ditch by the time we met him. I kept my bus steady, slowing down to a crawl, and the pickup kept fish-tailing toward us: . . . left, . . . right, . . . left, . . . right, . . . --the only thing keeping him from going in the ditch was he was perfectly straddling the high crown of the road--you know, the engineered crest to help the rain run-off. Finally, he was getting dangerously close, doing maybe 25mph, and I wondered if I was going to have to take to the ditch myself to avoid a head-on collision. Then, in the last few yards, the man made a miraculous recovery, straightened his pickup out . . . and slipped by us in his own lane at about 10mph, but white as a ghost. The little first-grade girl sitting in the right front seat looks up in the big mirror at me with her eyes bulging out . . . and says: "What was that all about?!" And I suppose I said something like, "It's all part of the show, folks, go back to your seats."

Anyway, good school-bus drivers enjoy having the kids around--I suppose I'm that way because I never had kids of my own (besides my books). But it's important to have control of your bus-load of kids . . . because you never know when there might be a possible emergency, where you need everybody's undivided attention and respect.

Possible School-Bus Emergencies

I don't mean to scare you, but all kinds of things can go wrong on or around a school bus. Besides the kids themselves possibly needing first-aid--for choking, epilepsy, bleeding, allergic reactions, and more,-- the whole bus could have some kind of trouble: accidents, fires, mechanical breakdowns, being stuck on rail-road tracks, or natural disasters including blizzards or flooding or downed power lines. Just figuring out whether or not to evacuate a bus-load of kids can be a nerve-racking decision.

So, . . . one of the trickier parts of being a school-bus driver is this: while you spend most of your job preventing and avoiding emergencies, . . . when an emergency finally does arise, you are expected to have control of your kids and know what to do johnny-on-the-spot. That can be tricky, when you consider it's not like a driver has a conditioned reflex for everything that could come along--let alone the total lack of respect from all angles. . . . EMTs and SWAT teams . . . in a way have it easier, . . . because they are constantly practicing what they're going to do in an emergency: EMTs are constantly doing CPR or stopping bleeding or dealing with allergic reactions; and SWAT teams are constantly practicing dealing with their difficult situations. And how often are the EMTs and SWAT teams the first on the scene?--not very often--while a school-bus driver is most-surely the first on the scene when his-r-her own bus has trouble.

Being a ski instructor and horse wrangler and

school-bus driver a lot of years, I have had countless First-Aid and CPR courses--I've dealt with a few injuries over the years, but I so far have never had to perform CPR on anyone, and I hope I never have to. Just because a person has been "trained" and done some practice--this doesn't mean they are going to have everything it takes if the life-or-death situation actually arises. We've got thousands of school-bus drivers out there who are not even up to par with the military sniper accustomed to just shooting paper targets. . . . Am I saying our school-bus drivers need more extensive training--no, not really. Most would agree one of the most important pieces of equipment on a school-bus is a two-way radio to keep in touch with the schools and bus barn. This is why, when I drove a preschool bus with eleven 3-to-5-year-olds, I used to get irritated when my coworkers always wanted me to do other busy-work things besides my job: forgetting the bus cell-phone or forgetting to unlock the bus's emergency door from the inside or forgetting to get fuel-- these seemingly small mistakes could all be extremely dangerous for the kids. . . . School-bus drivers aren't supposed to be paid for "how hard they work," we are paid for "how smart we work," much like that bored-silly "Maytag Repairman"--**it's more the trouble you don't see that we are paid for. . . . Then, if there is trouble, we'll have a plan, but we need all the support we can get.** Most people don't know it, but it is against the law in many states . . . for a school-bus fuel tank to be less than half full--it prevents a lot of unnecessary trouble. Yet, without going into detail here, your employer or school district should have a breakdown-and-accident procedure, posted somewhere smart in each bus, so that a driver can remember how to handle a situation. I've seen a number of these plans over the years, and they all have the right stuff on them, but they tend to be too complicated or hard to decipher in the heat of battle, with ten or twelve things on a list. So here is a simplified version.

SCHOOL-BUS BREAKDOWN/ACCIDENT PROCEDURE

1   **Stop Bus, <u>Assess Situation</u>**
     (move out of danger)
2   **Make <u>Evacuation Decision</u>**
     (last resort)***
3   **<u>Call for Help</u>**
     (radio or cell-phone)
4   **Protect Scene**
     (<u>flashers</u>, triangles)
5   **<u>First-Aid</u>--if necessary**
     (checklist in pocket)***
6   **Account for Passengers**
     <u>Roll Sheet</u>
7   **Cooperate with <u>Authorities</u>**

\#

I put my small First-Aid cheat-card here also, because, again, for myself being a writer, I guess I feel like all the first-aid books I've ever read . . . are not organized exactly right, so there's a lot of skipping around and an enormous amount to remember in no particularly logical order, . . . even though you're likely to only need a small percentage of it. The way I've wrangled the First-Aid scenarios was this: regular Health Emergencies, where you lay the victim on their side in the Recovery Position afterward, . . . and Accident scenarios, where you lay the victim on their back in the Shock Position afterward. The Health Emergencies, which may involve remembering your ABCs (Airway, Breathing, Circulation): half of them tend to befall people in poor health to begin with, like old folks; . . . and half of them tend to be more likely only in certain environments, but could happen to anybody, like a fireman or a wild teenager. Then the Accidents,

FIRST AID   +Transport

Emergencies--...Recovery Position
    Choking   Smoke, Asphyxiation
    Hrt Attck/CA Drowning
    Stroke (Brain) Electrocution   .
    Diabetes (ID) Ht Exhaustion/ Ht Stroke
  Epilepsy (ID)   Cold Exposure, Frost Bite
    Primary Assessment: Shake+Shout, 911
        Airway—finger sweep
          Breathing—2 rescue breaths
           5 abdominal thrusts (Heimlich Mnvr)
            Circulation—CPR 15c:2b; infant 5c:1b
Accidents--- . . . Shock Position
    Bleeding (**D**eadly)—pressure+elevation
     Internal Bleeding—like Shock
    Broken Bones, Spinal Injuries—immobilization
     Head Injuries—keep awake
    Burns—cold water, Shock
     Eye Injuries
    Poison, Snake Bite---no-cold
     Insect Bites+Stings—yes-cold, Epinephrine
     Allergies to foods or meds---Epinephrine

if you'll notice, each one more-or-less has its percentage of likelihood in different environments: burns and snake-bites shouldn't be likely on a school-bus, but a major crash with bleeding and broken bones could be; . . . but having a few kids with severe allergies to insect bites and stings or allergies to certain foods like peanuts . . . are high possibilities, the more kids you deal with--but the parents and teachers and the kids themselves usually tend to know who they are, and they are likely to carry their own Epinephrine-Pen to treat their own ensuing Anaphylaxic Shock.

I'm not saying everybody needs to follow what I say here; but, for me, when I break things down like this, into categories, I find that I can worry half as much, and then half-again, about what problems might arise. Again, about the only really-likely Health Emergencies you might have with kids . . . are the occasional student with epilepsy or diabetes or allergic reactions. They aren't likely to have a heart attack like an old person, and they shouldn't be likely to choke if you don't give them suckers to suck on during the ride, you can evacuate if there's smoke, and no one's likely to drown if you keep the bus out of the lakes and rivers, no one is likely to freeze on a bus, and you aren't likely to see any heat illness if you don't leave a kid on a hot bus-- you're probably more likely to see a downed power-line to stay away from, than you are many other scenarios, because of a crash or some natural disaster like an earth-quake or a wind-storm or an ice-storm.

(On the flip-side of my First-Aid card, I have myself a little Survival Guide, so I can remember some things in their order of importance, like Shelter, Water, Fire, Food. I won't put it in this book, as the schools will have their own idea of what belongs in their bus first-aid kits and so on. But you can find it in my *Heinsian BIKE-PACKING* manual. Basically, it's a good idea to never leave home without your jacket and some simple things in your pockets, like a small pocket-knife, a cigarette lighter to start fires with, even a few small bandages, . . . cigarettes, whiskey (just kidding), . . . and a plan, . . . in case the worst might happen--enjoy watching Anthony Hopkins in *The Edge*.)

Let me talk a minute about cooperating with other

authorities. People in Law Enforcement or Emergency Medical Training or on the Local Fire Department . . . tend to be more--how should I say?--cocky than your average school-bus driver. They like excitement, the like to take charge, and they can come across as a lot more confident than the average school-bus driver, even aggressive sometimes maybe. This is one of my quirks as a school-bus driver: I'm not as meek as most people come in thinking I would be--it almost stuns them when I get real assertive real quick when I have to, almost like Harrison Ford hiding out with the Amish People in the movie *Witness*. This may be why I sort of want to lateral the football to a few other younger, newer drivers. I've had sort of the same problem in Ski School: we ski instructors spend more time preventing trouble; then, when there is trouble, like a broken leg or a lost snow-boarder, the ski patrol can come in and save the day, just like the Marines landing on the beaches for France for D-Day (--don't be surprised if you see a Ski Patrolman by the name of Norman D. in one of my other books). . . . I hate to say it, but sometimes when there's an emergency or things go haywire, part of the human species is notorious for finding blame in others and looking for a scapegoat. I hope I am not that kind of a jerk, always blaming others and always looking for a scapegoat; on the other hand, I believe I have been a scapegoat a number of times in my life, always helping someone else look better. I guess I've reached a point in my life where I want to keep the people in charge honest--I don't have a lot of patience for people in power who aren't at least as good as the people they are controlling or ordering around.

One time, a friend of mine got T-boned by a small

car in her big bus. No one on the bus was injured really; but, when the city police showed up, they evacuated the bus in such a hasty way that, in a very short time, no one knew for sure what kid was where anymore--they did not allow her to do the parts of her job that she was perfectly capable of doing, especially concerning accountability of students, and it made more than a few parents panicky, and the driver became something of a scapegoat. This is why the roll-call sheet earlier in this chapter is so important--for a sub it may not be totally easy, but it's about as easy as we can make it, *if* it is done right by the people "above" the sub, like the regular driver and the transportation director.

I am reminded of an incident I had my first few weeks as a dude wrangler:

About six of us wranglers had been "legging-up" the dude string of about eighty horses for maybe a week, when the boss decided to let the kitchen and cabin girls go out with us for a nice leisurely ride around the ranch. They had me out in front, because the other wranglers had known each other longer, and so they were hanging back reminiscing. Something hardly noticeable was that one of the cabin girls' horse was a bit fidgety--it was sort of down-played because the girl was giggling and didn't seem bothered by it. I tried to tell her to keep her horse behind mine, but it didn't register too well for two reasons: being new and inexperienced, I wasn't that assertive, and I wasn't so much someone to look up to in her eyes. Well, ten minutes into the ride, it happened: her horse took off at a dead run. Well, my horse jumped around a bit--he was known for his strength and fire,--but I didn't want to make her horse go faster by chasing her, so I held back more at a slow trot or slow lope and tried to yell to her, "Turn your horse in a big circle!" Well, by now one of the more experienced wranglers from the rear came up to the front and ran out there with some good instruction, "Turn your horse in a big circle!" . . . Well, they made a big circle together, and he was finally able to get to her and grab her horse's bridle. . . . And I looked like a fool, and I felt about as guilty as a guy could feel. If that horse had gone under a low-hanging branch, she could have been killed.

Most agreed within an hour . . . that we all had a hand in it, Peggy's runaway--we had all been too complacent. It took me a few years to get over it. There I was: a new wrangler who admitted he was new, I had virtually no experience galloping in a safe arena let alone out in the pasture full of badger holes and timber, I'd never witnessed a runaway before, we hardly knew the horse Peggy was riding, and I hardly new the horse I was riding--and they had me out in front. Shame, Shame, Shame. I felt guilty about it for too many years, and I don't know that Peggy ever forgave me--but how could she know what all had transpired?

. . . Whenever my friend Dan Mortensen, seasoned dude wrangler and school-bus driver, is asked what to do in case of a runaway, he always starts with: "The best thing to do . . . is not have a runaway in the first place." . . . That's the same approach of a good school-bus driver: try to prevent having breakdowns, try to avoid having accidents, certainly prevent having a runaway down a mountain, try to prevent kids choking on candy, find out who's allergic to what--and that's a good start. Then you've got your plan. . . . Whether it's riding horses, driving a bus, riding the chair-lift with ski students, or even writing a book, I've always said, of my own personal occupations: "You've got to have <u>the ability to think on your seat.</u>"

Speaking of **preventing runaways**, that's one of the greatest reasons for the CDL-B or A licenses--in most states, if not all, they come with the ever-crucial Air-Brake Endorsement, which is why they are not handed out like candy. While I have no intention of teaching regular driving in this book, it wouldn't hurt to touch on the possibility of runaway buses, another possible emergency. It's been my observation that too many buses, mostly OTR buses, go downhill too fast--those heavily graveled runaway truck ramps you see on mountain passes are there for a reason.

The best way to prevent a runaway bus is this: go down the mountain in one lower gear than you can climb that same road in, and you should have your bus already-shifted into that gear before the downhill grade--and it's nice if the bus has a transmission re-tarder. A lot of buses that should have a lever-acti-vated retarder with four settings . . . don't have one. The next best thing is a one- or two-setting engine brake or "jake brake"--that's what you hear when a big truck comes down a hill into a town, as the engine revs real loud. The bad thing about engine brakes: they are outlawed in most towns and cities, because of their noise; but, the thing is, that's when big rigs need all the help they can get slowing down and stopping--it can be frighteningly difficult to stop a huge bus or truck without the help of an engine-brake or transmis-sion-retarder.

Since the late 1990s, too many buses have had a lot of parasitic technology added, making it harder for a driver to control speed simply by being in a low-enough gear. So a lot of your automatic-transmission buses unfortunately require the driver to ride the brake pedal somewhat, especially if there is not a good retarder handy--and there are two schools of thought on this downhill braking: some say to use "steady-light pressure," and others recommend using the "jab" method of braking. To me, it's a no-brainer: I subscribe to the "steady-light pressure" method of downhill braking, and I'll tell you why: "steady-light pressure" may get warm, but it does not make your brakes hot, and it doesn't deplete your all-important air-supply; the "jab" method, on the other hand, is hard on everything, as it depletes the air-supply, heats things up in a hurry, and, . . . the second you take your foot off the brake pedal, your bus can take off like a lead balloon from the top window of an office building. What I find interesting: the "jab" method of mountain descent is usually taught by high-ranking driver trainers who live in a flat place like Dallas, Texas.

You don't hear about runaway school buses that often, but charter buses may have it happen more often than we know about--as the driver usually isn't around to discuss it afterward. --Although here's an interesting tidbit: the split rear axle for high-n-low gear ranges was outlawed on school-buses in Colorado many years ago, because of a couple of deadly runaways. I drove many buses with that difficult feature at the start of my career in Wyoming--and I can tell you it took a knack to operate that little red electric knob on your stick shifter.

I wasn't going to put this next little story in here, but, hah, what the heck!--it's "No Holds Barred," right?

It was the last day of the ski season about 1987 at Jackson Hole Ski Area, an emotional for a ski instructor and other locals. I couldn't help but start drinking about 2 in the afternoon when some friends handed me a beer. Then about 5-pm, it was common practice to go to Wilson's Stage-Coach Bar, with a live band till 10-pm every Sunday evening--and I only lived a few blocks away. My plan was certainly not to start that early, and it was always to be well-done by 10pm when the bar would close--that meant I could still be up after 6-am for my school-bus route and still be legal: "Eight hours between bottle and throttle." . . . Well, as I was headed out the door of the Stage-Coach Bar at 10-pm, Vern Peterson, one of the legends of Jackson Hole Ski School was still in the party mood: "Hey, Heins, you got any beer at your place?" Before I knew it, we were sitting down at my place talking about ski teaching and which teachers we held in high regard--most specifically we talked for three hours . . . about the Phil and Steve Mahre "White-Pass Turn," how interesting it was, how tricky it was, and how it had very little redeeming value for the general public. . . . I don't think I got to bed until another couple of beers later, after 1-am; . . . then about 6:45-am, precisely the time I was supposed to be pulling out of the Bus Barn in my bus, I suddenly awoke, still drunk and panic-stricken: I called my boss immediately, and immediately he made it easy for me: "So you're calling in sick?--okay, we've got you covered."

. . . Because Knowles Smith had all his bases covered as a great Transportation Director, he already had JoAnn, our roving driver, already handling my route with precision. Instead of being caught with his underwear on the outside of his pants, he had a plan for the occasional "No Show" Driver. . . . Before my after-noon route, I talked with Knowles about the problem and the probability of seeking professional help. When I went to the "true professionals," before they even knew much of anything about me, I was "GUILTY!" . . . and there was "only one solution: never to have an-other drop the rest of your life!" "Wait, wait, wait, hold on!" I said; and then the guy gave me a test: he said, "If you can go thirty days having three beers a day every day . . . but never a fourth, then you're probably okay." I took that challenge, and, by God, I made it! . . . That's been over twenty-two years ago, and I've probably had some slip-ups since then, but none that ever got in the way of my driving. . . . One time, driving for Ramblin' Express to the casinos in Cripple Creek, Colorado, I found myself an hour late for a run because I had set my clock back one-hour a day too early to "fall-back" from Day-light Saving Time--but that would have made my twenty-three hours early, right? . . . I guess the main point of this story is this: of all the people in-volved, Transportation Director Knowles Smith han-dled me the best, as well or better than those famous Horse Whisperers who know how to give their horses the benefit of the doubt. I think Knowles was sur-prised there was only that one time--it wasn't easy bal-ancing one of the wildest professions, ski instructor, . . . with one of the tamest, school-bus driver, especially in wild-n-wooly Jackson Hole. If I haven't done so al-ready, I nominate Knowles Smith as the Greatest School-Bus Transportation Director Ever, and I nomi-nate JoAnn Camenzind as the Greatest School-Bus Driver Ever.

Okay, let's do another Post-Trip Inspection for stow away kids before moving on to the next chapter--be sure to look under the seats.

Anatomy of
an **Activity Trip**
or **Field Trip**

We now move out of the realm of the more obvious school-bus driving . . . and into the realm of taking groups of kids on long trips. With the kindergarten and elementary-age kids, the average field trip is probably no more than ten or twenty miles away; with middle-schoolers, you could be talking a couple of hundred miles away, to places like Denver's Natural History Museum, or the U.S. Mint; and, with High-Schoolers, I've had ten-day trips with them, more than a thousand miles away. Interestingly enough, I'd say most of my field trips and athletic activity trips were driven under the hat of Over-the-Road Bus Driver, not as a School-Bus Driver--but, any way you look at it, I've had thousands of day trips with school kids.

It's kind of funny really, how I acquired most of my experience as a trip driver. When I lived in Pueblo, Colorado, there was a shortage of school-bus drivers, and so I applied and went in for an interview. I had a number of years experience by then and seemed a bit too cocky to the interviewer: he wanted to make me jump through a whole bunch of unnecessary hoops close to the end of the school year for one month of work and pay me like a first-year driver with no experience, and I told him that wouldn't be acceptable; not too far into the interview, he slammed his notebook shut and announced: "All right, interview's OVER!" . . . A few weeks later, I started driving for TNM&O Coaches, and guess what happened for the next six years: since the schools had a shortage of drivers, they had to hire us to do most of their trips for them, at double the pay.

BEWARE!
Non-Pros . . . Masquerading As Drivers
  --Teachers & Coaches Doubling As Drivers
    Before we even get on the road, I should point out a scary scenario that's all too common in some school districts across the nation that are maybe too desperate for "saving money" (while the administrators are sure to get more than their fair share). You would think that, when there's a long trip to be made, it would naturally be assigned to a person hired to do the job. But, every now and again, you hear of an informal trip made by a teacher or a coach or even a parent in charge of a small club or team. You see them out and about from time to time . . . and think nothing of it: it may be a half-dozen students per vehicle who are members of the chess club or a small ski team or something like that, and they would be riding in 14-passenger school vans or smaller, maybe 9-passenger Chevy Suburbans (including the driver), or something else exempt from being classified for the operator to need a CDL or any Passenger Endorsement--then there's no need for a Log Book either.
    I hadn't really thought much about this scenario before, but, one day I couldn't help but get wind of it: Sometimes a driver gets assigned a trip, and then it

gets cancelled, and you just shrug your shoulders. Then you find out a week later that the trip was in-fact made, only it was made without a bus and bus driver. I don't know that it saves money so much, since a half-dozen smaller vehicles are required to take the place of a bus. And I don't know if the coaches and teachers are paid extra to drive or not, or if they just do it out of the "kindness of their heart," . . . but I wonder if there's strong incentive or reimbursement of some kind. It could boil down to the basic shortage of bus drivers-- they simply need a driver for something else more urgent that day. I don't have a problem so much with parents driving their own kids and friends on a trip, because they can relax and be "Off Duty" during the event, while that's when a coach or teacher is supposed to really go to work.

Think about it: there's an event in the big city 250-miles away that goes from 8am to 5pm. And, in order to save money, or if they don't have a bus or professional driver available, they have the teacher or coach drive instead--in fact, there may be a half dozen vehicles with a half-dozen teachers or coaches driving them. Well, each driver has a good four- or five-hour drive to get down there, so you know they have to start driving probably before 4am. Then they supervise the group all day from 8 to 5 in their real profession. . . . And then, counting dinner for the students somewhere on the road, that driver is lucky to be back to the school parking lot by 10pm or later. That's an eighteen-hour day for coaches and teachers, with no layover, which they will agree is pretty darn rough--and it's even rougher knowing they are not even trained as professional drivers. . . . Further, the true professional drivers, who would be safely be on **Layover** during the event, are cheated out of work that is rightfully theirs.

In this "wing-it" type of scenario, **complacency is key**, and the dangers run rampant. When there's an extraordinarily-tough chore like this to be done, marathon driving and coaching, who's first to volunteer?--the tough guy with the big ego. Then peer pressure creeps in, as the tough guy might have to pressure some meek colleague into being just as tough, like an assistant coach or a fellow teacher, to drive the other van or something. At take-off time, a driver's seat may not even be in adjustment, and you can almost guarantee the mirrors aren't adjusted. Those 14-passenger vans scare me: besides having a tired overworked aggressive non-pro driver behind the wheel, they quite often get loaded to the max, with every seat a passenger, then several-pounds of gear with each passenger, and maybe even a good-sized cargo trailer hooked onto the rear bumper. Then you can bet, out of the several passengers, there's probably a couple of BSDLs, Back-Seat Driver's Licenses. You see these trips out on the Interstate Highways, with a youthful gleam about them--maybe you play leap-frog with them for a couple-hundred miles, if you can keep up, because their prestigious event, or just getting home quicker, is always more important than any driving plan.

Just check your news stories. A lot of your most horrific auto crashes . . . involve those 14-passenger vans driven by non-professional drivers. I'm reminded of a van like this on I-40 in New Mexico around the turn of the millennium: it rear-ended a semi-trailer temporarily pulled-over on the shoulder of the road--to get a body count, they probably had to count all the legs or feet . . . and divide by two. Safety ain't even an afterthought in a deal like that. So, even with a lot fewer passengers, more people can die in one of those vans . . . than in a 55-passenger motor coach.

That said, let's get on . . . to the way trips really should be handled, in my opinion.

Pre-Planning, Pacing-n-Rhythm

A good half-hour or so before the spot-time, the driver will show up at the bus-barn to pre-trip his bus and to get settled in with his seat and mirrors in adjustment. A good bus will be accommodating to the driver, having a place for him to put his personal belongings--this is especially needed for the longer trips. If a bus does not have a luggage rack or compartment above or behind the driver, he may need to use the passenger seat directly behind him to store his small brief-case, travel bag, toiletries, and maybe a coffee thermos and a few snacks. Everyone concerned should understand this, including the Transportation Director and the Trip Leaders--there's nothing worse than a new driver showing up for a trip . . . and a trip leader telling him "your stuff is in the way." This kind of unwelcome greeting is not likely to happen to a "soccer mom" type of driver who may be the wife of the coach she is driving; but it still shouldn't happen to a strange new face that no one is in love with yet.

A lot of schools don't think about this stuff like a real charter company, but there should be a spot-time and a departure-time; the spot-time is fifteen minutes before departure-time. This fifteen-minute buffer-time gives everyone a chance to move at a slower safer pace; it gives everyone a chance to not forget something important as they have a little time to think. Drinking water is a pretty important item on long drives, especially in the hotter areas, but this falls more under the jurisdiction of the trip leaders than of the bus driver--a minor mechanical breakdown for a few hours out in the desert without water can be deadly.

Sometimes, the Transportation Director or the Dispatcher or a fellow driver . . . will fore-warn a trip driver about some problematic idiosyncrasies of a particular group. One time, hauling the track team, the dispatcher warned me about the pole vaulters loading their 15-ft-long poles through the roof vents of the bus: "They don't need risk breaking their neck climbing on the roof," she said, "they can angle their poles in through the main door." The next day after the track-meet, I told her, "Sure enough, before I knew what was going on, there was a pole-vaulter on the roof, trying to load poles through the roof vent like you warned me." Then I livened the story up a bit: "Soon as I found out he was up there, I took him for a spin around the parking lot to teach him a lesson." Of course, the Dispatcher gasped and said, "You didn't!" So I embellished the story some more: "But I couldn't find any low-hanging branches or anything, so he got off easy." . . . Of course I didn't haul any high-school kid around on the roof-top of a trip bus--I mean, I don't want to go to jail or get charged with manslaughter or anything,-- but it was a fun story, . . . only she, being somewhat new to the school district, actually believed me there for awhile, until I reassured her that some of what this writer says . . . is double-reverse hyperbole or under-statement. Stories like this are part of my attempt to show that drivers are human . . . and have a human element to them, unlike most buses.

A lot of groups of people seem to think the bus driver isn't that far removed from the bus itself--they think the driver is there to be turned on or off at will just like the bus itself. They think the pace and rhythm of a trip is of no concern to the driver, because the driver is not the customer--and the customer's always right, right? The Question arises: **Which comes first: the Group? or the Driver?**

Granted, some trips are easy: go thirty miles, stay four hours, and thirty miles back; but, when the miles or hours in the day start adding up, the comfort of the driver is of utmost concern, for the safety of everyone. Most school trips are day trips or evenings, . . . and the day should be somewhat planned in advance--there can be some flexibility, as long as it doesn't get out of hand and tax the driver's patience. With respect for the driver, as well as everyone else including babysitters or pet-sitters, there should be some kind of plan for: when the trip starts, arrival time at destination, how long at destination . . . and what time to start home, approximate time arriving home.

Before the trip takes off, or at least just as the trip starts rolling, the driver needs a list of passengers--that's pretty standard. The longer the trip, and maybe the younger the kids, the more the need for this list. If anything were to happen to that bus, the authorities and family and friends will want to know in a hurry exactly who's on that bus. Getting this list should be simple: the coaches or teachers leading the group can have a ready-made list, or they can have the driver circulate a clip-board for everyone to sign. But getting this passenger list can be like pulling teeth; and even if you get it, it too often is not even accurate: the coaches or teachers need to check the list making sure their own names are on it, and get an accurate count of passengers--then it wouldn't hurt for the driver to add his own name separate from the passengers. When a driver requests this passenger list, give it to him, and don't treat him like he's putting unnecessary demands on the trip leaders. . . . Driving home obviously, there are often fewer passengers, as some kids ride home instead with parents; the driver could use an asterisk by those names, designating they are not on board for the return trip.

Sometimes, even just before a trip takes off, there could be a choice about which road to take. One way may be too hilly-n-windy or too snowy for a huge bus--there may even be a bridge half-way that has a weight-limit that the bus would be illegal and dangerous crossing. Usually one way is longer but faster, while the other way is shorter but slower; but what's true for a small car may not be true for a big bus. The driver may know some good information, or he may have questions. Most good drivers are open to going on just about any road the passengers want, but they may have a good reason for not wanting to take a road:

I went to pass a slow pick-up one night on a big open Indian Reservation road; before I knew it, there was a car coming head-on over a little hill, so I had to back the bus off in a hurry. I noticed the oncoming car slowed down pretty well also, and it didn't honk at me like I thought it would. It was a minor close call, and it was kind of embarrassing; but, on looking back, there was not solid yellow line, and there was no sign indicating a No-Passing Zone--that's how American Indian roads can be. So looking back further, if we had not dawdled at dinner, we wouldn't have been on this fifty-mile road in the dark; or we could have taken the US Highways. And, looking back ever further, I think the coaches I was with knew this peculiarity about Indian Roads in the area; but they didn't find it necessary to let me in on their secret. . . . For what it's worth, Indian Roads often have Indian ponies roaming freely too--I've had coaches get irritated with me for not going the speed limit when there was a bunch of innocent horses around.

Then it wouldn't hurt to start a trip by asking the driver's professional opinion about where to take **breaks** and when, for the safety and comfort and well-being of all the passengers . . . and the driver. It's true that the Passenger Endorsement on a Bus Driver's CDL means he understands and tries to address the needs of the passengers; but a driver has to address his own needs as well concerning potty-breaks, food, fatigue, timing, and so on--this is a lot easier for say a truck driver who doesn't have fifty customers breathing down his neck every mile of the way. Some drivers can wing it and be totally spontaneous like a fighter-jet pilot or a NASCAR race-car driver, which the coaches and passengers may love, but it is unsafe to assume every driver should be this way. For some drivers, it's the not-knowing . . . of any possible breaks in sight . . . that can stress them out-- you shouldn't have to drive in a fog, especially when it's a sunny day.

There is such a thing as **too many breaks**, which can wear a driver out with too much starting and stopping, more red lights, more shifting, more tight parking lots to negotiate. Then there is **too long of a stretch without a break**, which may not only be hard on the driver but on some meek passengers as well--it's not uncommon for an aggressive coach to selfishly demand pressing on, especially if his poor planning has made the bus get behind schedule. I don't know how many times I've had a coach or group leader pressure me two-thirds of the way there by asking "Can you get us there by 5?" which may be faster than the speed limit will allow. . . . And the least obvious is the **ill-timing of breaks**, like twenty minutes into a long three-hour stretch, . . . or not letting a tired driver break just before the forty-five minutes of hell in metropolitan traffic. Local information, if anybody knows, about avoiding rush-hour traffic can sure go a long way. Then, when there is a break, it should be agreed upon beforehand how long that break will be--don't tell a driver and twenty minutes and then have it turn into an hour, and don't tell a driver it will be an hour and then tell him to hop-to after only forty minutes. If no one cares, it is not uncommon for the driver to be last in line for the rest-room and/or the food line, because he usually needs to be the last one off the bus.

When you do park the bus for a break, as I mentioned concerning parking at the bus barn, try to park the bus so that it will "settle in" and not be dependent on the parking brake. Even if you have a little slope, if you park across the slope, with the wheels turned uphill, then you won't have to worry about the parking-brake knob getting bumped and coming undone, and you won't have to make a big project out of wheel-chocking. Parking this safe-n-easy way may take a few extra seconds, so you might have to tell the trip leader what you're up to.

A little advice to some of the newer bus-drivers out there: once you have your CDL-B-PS and the rest of the credentials that allow you to drive a big bus full of people, now the fun begins. In a way, you know just enough now . . . to get yourself and everyone around you into trouble: whereas the other CDL drivers without passengers have the luxury of taking their time and learning the real world at a slower pace, you're learning two huge things at the same time and sooner than you might want--the real world . . . and the unauthorized, unqualified, dysfunctional, ignorant, and egotistical . . . people on your bus. Remember, they don't have the credentials and authority that you have, and they may even have ulterior motives, so they will invariably and inadvertently . . . ask you and even tell you . . . to do things with that bus that are not in anyone's best interest.   Fortunately, most school buses are forty feet long, with a nimble wheel-base and plenty of ground clearance and a fair amount of room overhead; but you might have access to a forty- or forty-five-foot bus that is extremely tall and extremely low to the ground with the longest wheel-base possible--you have to know how to look into the future a little bit . . . to keep you and your big bus out of trouble. With the huge buses (described more in the chapter on Greener Highways), you can easily hit more tree branches and things like street signs and motel canopies with the height of the bus, you will have more trouble just turning in tight places, and you have a good chance of bottoming-out and even getting hung-up on some normal city streets and parking lots because of the low ground-clearance.

When a group or trip leader is hungry or tired or excited about their event, they will often have tunnel vision about what restaurant or motel parking lot to pull into--and they might not even be awake when they tell you to pull in somewhere risky. All too often, a group leader will suggest a driver to pull in somewhere at the last possible second, . . . or after the last possible second. An inexperienced less-assertive driver could easily make a hasty maneuver, even with an easy bus, changing lanes without having enough time before a turn or intersection, . . . and have a wreck.

And they don't realize that, for a careful less-hasty driver, turning a big bus around can be quite a project: in a town, it is likely you have to go around a city block, and sit at a couple of red lights; in the country, you might have to go several miles to find a safe turn-around. "One thing I've learned driving big buses," I tell them: "two wrongs don't make a right, . . . but three lefts do."

When you get that Passenger Endorsement, they basically want to know if you care about the passengers; they don't warn you about the passengers not being endorsed or properly trained to order you around or give you directions. Most unsuspecting new-and-innocent drivers . . . have a few close calls, and then they get tough and learn to watch out for themselves. (Man, I wish this book had been out when I was a new driver--you new guys don't know how lucky you are.)

One time, with a group of World War II veterans having a reunion, the leader told me to pull into a rest area at the last possible second. It was an Interstate, and there was no one close behind me, so I went ahead and did it, but I had to brake hard as we got into it, and the group was a little surprised. "Kind of like landing a fighter plane on an air-craft carrier, huh?" I said to him, as he had a sheepish look on his face; and then I corrected myself: "No, more like a C-130 cargo plane," and he smiled. Then I added, "No extra charge, folks, it's all part of your trip." Sometimes, for the passengers, it's hard for them to sort out what's bad driving . . . or what's just bad directions.

One time, in Portland, Oregon, the group leader told me to "Follow that van." We got out on the freeway, and, before I knew it, the van had ditched me. We couldn't find them anywhere, . . . so I took an exit ramp an parked for quite a few minutes until the group got their plan in order. I always carry an Atlas when I'm driving, but it's always nice if the driver knows where he's going before you get into heavy traffic. I don't know if you've ever been to Portland, Oregon, with its waterways and hills and bridges and clouds galore not far from the Ocean--it ain't as easy as driving in Denver or Salt Lake City on a sunny day with big mountain ranges and a few more sky-scrapers to help keep you oriented.

. . . Okay, that's en-route; now we need to talk about **layover**. Don't forget: when there are large groups of people involved going to various types of activities or events: too often the bus drivers are expected to stand around or shuttle around or twiddle there thumbs "enjoying" what all the group is so excited about--some drivers are kept up for more than twelve hours at a stretch . . . without access to a resting area, which ought to be a "Do-Not-Disturb"-Sign motel room, . . . before being required to drive a few hundred miles again starting at a time of night when most are used to going to bed. This is why I say it so important to understand: the bus driver is Not "On Vacation," he's "On Vocation." Even if a driver has a motel room during a long layover, that's no guarantee he can sleep exactly when the group wants him to-- and it's not uncommon for him to be disturbed by a passenger or two when he is asleep, "because we need to get something off the bus." And, Administrators, even if a driver is in a motel sleeping, all but maybe eight hours in a twenty-four-hour period should be compensated for, since he's not exactly able to be home doing what he wants. If a driver gets to visit with family or friends while on a trip, this should not be considered as part of the compensation, and a good driver knows how to not let this interfere with his duties--the best charter companies know this. Sometimes, in the school-bus trip arena, if the driver is related to the passengers or coaches or teachers, there's too much of a "Soccer-Mom" mentality running the show, and the true-professional drivers are not noticed for their dedication.

One more thing about trip drivers. While they look like they have it easy standing around or even lounging around at the destination point, when the trip started, the driver was the first one out of bed, . . . and when the trip ends, he's the last one to bed. And there could be another trip assigned to him hanging over his sleep time just eight hours around the corner. So it's important to understand **how a driver's days may be linked together**. This is some behind-the-scenes stuff that the passengers and coaches may not know about or even consider . . . unless the Transportation Director passes this information along. It's too awkward for the driver to have to bring this up at the last minute, "raining on everyone's parade" to get a return leg started home on time; he needs the support of some more of those in charge, and way back before the trip even gets started. Even for a lot of less-busy school-bus drivers, this may not bother or concern them if they only get one trip a week; but, for drivers who do a lot of trips, this is of utmost importance. There are just too many people from all angles treating drivers in a condescending manner assuming that every driver "has it easy."

I took a fair number of trips to the Flyin' W Chuck-Wagon Dinner and Cowboy Singing near Colorado Springs. A handful of singing cowboys and kitchen help can handle about a thousand guests per evening feeding them barbecued beef or chicken, a baked potato, some baked beans, apple-sauce, and lemonade or iced tea. They do it most efficiently, military style, or like a big ranch handling a thousand head of cattle: get 'em in, and get 'em out, about a half-hour to get everyone served. In about a two-hour dinner and show, they make money hand-over-fist, selling CDs and T-shirts and all kinds of souvenirs as well; yet, whenever I showed up as a bus driver, one of maybe a half-dozen each night, they always expected us to help serve the guests. I never expected them to park my bus for me, so they shouldn't expect me to do their work for them.

Sure, they give the drivers a free meal, but they shouldn't expect us to work for it--in fact, we are already working for it, by being a professional driver in the grand scheme of things. If it were a school-bus driver, they never considered that maybe that driver has a route to do at 5-o'clock the next morning; and a trip driver could have an assignment a bit tougher than that, before and after. If they don't want to give a bus-driver a "free" meal, throw the left-overs in the garbage instead, fine: I'll drive to Denny's during the layover, if I can get the bus out of the parking lot, which I probably can't--and packing a meal is not nearly as easy for an away-from-home trip driver as it might be for a factory worker with the same schedule every day.

I like what Grandma Ivy says to George Strait in the movie *Pure Country*, when he scolds her for coming to a concert but not letting him know she was going to be there: "No, you were workin', and you don't disturb a man . . . when he's workin'."

Speaking of the Flyin' W, Jackson Hole had the same exact business when I was there, the Bar J Chuck-Wagon, and it was owned by Babe Humphrey, who happened to be an old school-bus driver. And Bill Soper sure could sing "Blue Prairie"--and what a nice contrast to a yellow school bus. Maybe, if the Flyin' W Wranglers had sang "Blue Prairie," like the Bar J Wranglers, I might feel different.

. . . So it is wise to do some pre-planning for a

trip, and the driver's should have a big say in the pre-planning--they don't call me "Itinerar' Gar'" for nothing. You've got the group's needs and de-sires, and you've got the driver's needs--it would be nice if they can all overlap. If the itinerary doesn't consider the driver's needs, it can be a bit scary. Whenever there is a big bus crash on na-tional news, where ten people get killed, it's usu-ally this behind-the-scenes stuff that went unad-dressed--and the driver isn't usually around any-more to talk about it, and he's the scapegoat. So, for a driver to raise his hand early with a sugges-tion about the pacing-n-rhythm of a trip, or to re-quire respect during lay-over, he's only thinking of the Safety of the Trip in general--he's not trying to be selfish. The pacing of trips is of utmost impor-tance on most trips when you consider it all adds up in a driver's day-in-day-out, month-after-month, many-year-long career.

A lot of people don't think about this, but . . . school-bus drivers never work for tips, though they may get friendly favors or more special treatment from some coaches or someone in the administration, . . . and charter-bus drivers very-often work for tips--this can effect how drivers perform their job, how much they'll bend over backwards or bend the rules and what-not, so the money or the perks can taint some of the common-sense safety issues. Drivers who put their own ba-sic needs aside often wear-out sooner and die younger--getting nerve damage in their hands, hurting their eyesight because they forgot their sunglasses, even losing kidneys after so much bumpity-bump,--and that's not good bus business. And the lenient drivers, who are always deemed "nice" by the customers, make it harder for other drivers to get their needs met. It's one thing to give good friendly service to your groups; it's quite another to sacrifice your total health and happiness for their selfish wants.

In fact, far too many full-time professional trip drivers are in poor physical condition, especially the ones that take trips full-time; and it's hardly their own fault, since they are overworked and out-numbered by the Status-Quo, and their whole Arcadian Rhythm is out of balance. When they are on layover, they are of course expected to take it easy, to not overexert themselves. When they are home between trips, they may not have time to go exercise, because of the lack of time between trips. The more-part-time casual trip drivers are usually in healthier shape, because they have more of their time to themselves, but they won't know what the full-time trip drivers are going through.

I used to think "Don't confuse school-bus drivers with OTheR drivers," but I think I'll retrack that. We all have the same needs for safety and making a living. But, when I drove with those thousands of OTR drivers, I could tell which ones had never driven a school bus . . . or which ones had never taken a Defensive-Driving Course . . . or which ones had never stopped to consider where the drivers fit in to the hierarchy. Each type of driver can learn from the others.

School Buses, by most state laws, are not supposed to go faster than 65-mph--this is a good rule for safety. I don't know how many times I've seen trips planned by basketball coaches who did the same trip last year in their car at 80-mph and no breaks--they just naturally assume the bus driver can match that or even beat it. If a bus driver so much as forgets to stop at a Rail-Road Track, he is subject to losing his Commercial Driver License. Another common state law is that the school-trip bus is supposed to stop for a break at least every two hours--this is probably more for the group than for the driver, because, if a driver is feeling good, he may want to drive for three-hours straight. Now, school buses have these rules and laws governing them, mostly to protect the students, but the big tour buses have more freedom-- the big non-school motor coaches can legally go faster than 65mph and don't have to stop every two hours, but they do have a rest-room on board and more comfortable seats, and these drivers are more likely permitted to sip on a cup of coffee or diet coke as they go. So groups and drivers have to consider which type of bus they are going in. If a school district hires a big charter outfit, that bus is not so subject to school policies and procedures; but, if a school district owns a fancy charter bus, it can become a gray area about which rules apply--

the bus itself may not even be legal, if it doesn't have all the school requirements involving things like pedestrian mirrors and so on.

I thought it interesting one day, when the annual School-Bus Inspectors showed up to inspect all our buses--that is, all except our "Big Red," because it was not a school bus. Meanwhile, when I crossed state lines with that bus, I never knew if I was exempt from pulling into Port of Entries or not, because it was not a charter bus, it was a school trip bus. One day, I pulled into the Port and couldn't find the bus registration or insurance papers--somehow the soccer coach talked our way out of it; but, if a big charter bus didn't have all its paper-work in order, there would be hell to pay. It seemed our big luxury bus was exempt from being subject to school-bus laws, because it wasn't a school bus; and yet it seemed it was exempt from the same laws governing big charter buses, because it was own by a school rather than a charter-bus company--something seemed very fishy. . . . It's not my intention here to get bogged down in a debate about legal equipment and red-tape--I just wish to see more drivers and more groups and more administrators and more parents . . . be on the same sheet of music. And give more credit where credit is due . . . **rather than just making sure everyone's *"t's"* are dotted and *eyes* are crossed.**

If it's a fairly small school district with only a few thousand residents in town, chances are the normal yellow school buses should be used on trips--and I've seen a good many bona-fide school-buses treated with a fancy paint job to become a nice trip bus showing the team pride. It takes a pretty big school to warrant chartering a big motor coach from an outside company; and it takes a pretty big school to warrant buying a big luxuri-ous motor coach of its own (like Prevost, MCI, Van Hool, Setra, Eagle) even used--you've got to have enough groups going enough places enough days of the year, otherwise the bus is not earning its keep.

Oh, well, no matter which jurisdiction of buses or drivers, . . . I wish more groups could appreci-ate **Enjoying the Trip** for the trip's sake. That's why a lot of bus drivers drive buses--we like to get around and look at the country-side. Most people subscribe to the notion that the travel time is a curse; they can't wait to get there, they can't wait to get home, and they pressure the driver with this unhealthy attitude--of course, a percentage of drivers can't enjoy the trip either.

You take a trip through Northern Arizona, through the Navajo country, or through rural Montana with beautiful ranch country, and all the coaches see is gloom, and they pass this attitude on to the kids; you drive a tour bus through the same country with a bus-load of German tourists, and all they see is the beauty. That's part of my problem working for small schools where most of the people have barely been outside the county--they don't know what all is out there, and they may not be interested in it. In my ski-teaching and horse-wrangling and OTR bus-driving careers, I've had the opportunity to meet more types of people than I can count. You show up in a small school district after all that experience, and the local teachers, coaches, and other drivers still think it's your first rodeo. It becomes a rank thing with them, a pecking order, who's the best driver and what-not--"My uncle's done most to the varsity trips here since 1957, so who are you?" and that kind of thing, immediately making a driver feel out of place. I mention this here, not because I want to talk about the OTR business prematurely, but because it effects the ability of a small school district to carry out their trips fairly, smoothly, and safely--the drivers are more likely relatives, and some of the professional aspects of the job go out the window.

When you show up at a school . . . in an outside-company charter bus, it's a different story, as they treat you with more respect. In the booming economic times of the 1990s, there was a lot more hiring of outside charter buses for school trips. The Country's Economy has a lot to do with the safety of the transportation business. Most of my school trips, interestingly enough, were not done under the guise of school-bus driver, but rather under the guise of charter-bus driver. I hauled countless grade-schoolers to the Denver Zoo, middle-schoolers to the Museum of Natural History, high-schoolers to a cadaver-lab in Phoenix, we went to huge butterfly exhibits, and huge oceanic aquariums, the list goes on--it's sort of a great way to get unlimited education.

I hauled the Salida, Colorado, High School football team to all their games and the state championship in the late '90s. After one particularly tense close game, one of the cheerleaders asked me if I got to see it. "Me watch the game? I got news for you: did you see that Number 89 catch those three touch-down passes in the fourth-quarter?--that was me." . . . The last game of the season, the championship game, they had me hauling the band instead of the team. The young band director, fresh out of college, was sitting in the seat right behind me talking about how, "if some of these high-schooler kids don't shape up, they're going to end up driving a bus." I got back at him though: when we were loading and unloading the band instruments under the bus, I would stand on the sidewalk by the biggest drum he had . . . and say, "How 'bout a drum roll?"

Every so often, a group might enjoy the trip too much. One group I had--I think it was a high-school group--actually sang all ninety-nine verses of "Ninety-nine Bottles of Beer On the Wall"--that has to be a record.

To sum things up about trip-driving for school, the tricky part goes back to the overall lack of re-spect from the teachers and coaches and admini-stration. The driver has the most amount of re-sponsibility . . . while receiving the least amount of respect. Sometimes the coaches don't even want to make the three-hundred-mile trip home on the bus after a long track meet or tournament--they would rather stay in a motel with their spouse or something like that,--but someone is required to ride along on account of the school kids need a chaperone, especially mixed high-schoolers late at night. If a driver suggests getting some parents to help out, then there is some red-tape as to the fact that none of them have the State Finger-print Clearance Card. Meanwhile, last I heard, the Charter Company drivers aren't required to have that card.

Okay, it's been a long trip, but there's one more thing I need to mention before we drop you readers off for the night. When I pull in to a town or parking lot late at night after a long drive, one of my pet-peeves is being asked to turn-on the interior lights of the bus a couple of blocks ahead of time and get a bunch of passengers rustling in the aisle, drop-ping bags on each other's heads. I know a lot of drivers do it as "a courtesy," or they are just suc-cumbing to unnecessary pressure, but nowhere in DOT or School-Bus guidelines does it suggest that a driver drive with interior lights on. As far as I am concerned, it is unsafe, as all the light reflects on the inside of the windshield, making it difficult to see out for pedestrians, parked cars, and what-not, and the passengers can stay seated like they're supposed to for another thirty seconds. Why ruin a several-hundred-mile-trip with a hasty maneu-

ver right at the very end caused by too much mus-
cle from a passenger at the precise moment when a
driver is most fatigued?

Some Transportation Directors don't know this,
but: trip buses get dirty, especially on the inside. There
needs to be some kind of plan for dealing with bus-
cleaning without making it a miserable guilt-ridden
chore. I've seen Transportation Directors and some
drivers lay down lots of strict rules concerning passengers eating on the bus, in hopes of keeping buses spotless forever-and-ever, Amen--but the fact remains: the
passengers want to enjoy the trip as much as they can,
and buses get dirty as a result, just like a restaurants
and cafes. I'm not sure it's even that reasonable to ask
students to pick up their trash after midnight coming
back from a long trip, when they are still half asleep.
Then the last thing a driver needs to do is spend an
hour in the middle of the night cleaning a bus. . . . No,
trip-bus cleaning should be a routine affair scheduled
the next morning after a trip: whether it's the driver or
someone else in the bus barn, they could easily be paid
an hour for the bus interior alone . . . to pick-up trash,
sweep, mop, and even wash windows; the bus exterior
could take half as long and may or may not be necessary.

Let's do a Post-Trip Inspection . . . and park this
trip bus. Don't worry about cleaning it right now--
we'll have someone at the bus barn clean it tomorrow.
Meanwhile, let's get a good night's sleep before checking out the big OTR buses tomorrow.

Some SBDs 'Graduate' to Greener Highways

Yes, this book is mainly about school-bus driv ing, the unsung heroes; but it was first conceived as a book about Over-The-Road Bus Driving--it's pretty romantic and interesting in its own right . . . and deserves a chapter here, since a lot of school-bus drivers end up going this route, to make a higher paycheck. I think this chapter is highly necessary for any school-bus drivers thinking of "moving up" to the big buses, so they know what they might be getting into (besides the less-romantic school trips I mentioned in the last chapter). And it's a good chapter for helping School-Bus Trip Drivers take a step back to look at their own profession from a lot more angles. Except for a few routine deals out there, you can forget about having a home life, or being with your spouse or significant other as often as you'd like--although I noticed some guys doing it for just that reason, to get away from the spouse more often. And it can be hard on the body and digestive system if you don't have routine meal-times and sleep, as well as your mental health and spirit--I gained thirty pounds during my six-year stint, and got pretty grumpy and discour-aged sometimes. What got me through most of that time was I had a great boss, the most under-standing guy of dozens of drivers' needs at the same time (and I'll tell you about Neil Byrne later).

Line-Haul versus **Charters**, or Both

In this world, you've got **line-haul drivers**, like regular Greyhound Drivers, . . . **charter drivers**, who do day-trips or month-long trips and every kind of trip in between, . . . and "**Extra-Board**" **Drivers** (like I was), who go any place at any time for any reason. An Extra-Board Driver is like a Substitute without quite as much Substitute Syndrome--in fact, they may command more respect than regular drivers because they are the ones who really tie the whole big-bus industry together. Another type of bus driver here would be those guys who drive country-music sangers all over the country on their annual tours. Each type of driving has its interesting aspects--let's look at each one. With the big buses able to carry 200- to 300-gallons of fuel, getting from 6- to 12-mpg, it's a pretty efficient way to move big groups of people around.

Greyhound is the most obvious **line-run** company in the U.S., but they aren't the only one. Some of you may remember TrailWays, or Continental TrailWays, which used to be fairly big. A more obscure name would be like Powder River Bus Lines out of Wyoming. The company I worked for for six years was Texas, New Mexico, & Oklahoma Coaches, a subsidiary of Greyhound since the 1930s, which looks like Greyhound only doesn't say Greyhound. At any rate, these lesser-known bus companies could be linked up with Greyhound in the vast network of scheduled runs all over the nation.

It breaks my heart now, but there used to be a

lot more buses running through a lot more little
towns in the 1940s, '50s, and '60s. You see rem-
nants of bus travel's more-golden years--whole
cafeterias in places like Lubbock, Texas, that are
shut down now because of a lower quality of life.
When you go into a McDonald's next to a smaller-
town bus terminal and find the hot-water not
working in the rest-room, chances are they've
turned it off deliberately to discourage bus passengers from taking spit baths or shaving. Back
in the 1950s, riding a bus across the country was
not looked down upon--at the cafeterias in the
bus terminals, waitresses actually waited on you
cheerfully. In the 1990s, I noticed a lot of your
long-distance bus travelers couldn't afford a decent motel room along the way. Part of the
problem with bus-travel nowadays is that the depots are not always in the most convenient part
of town anymore, because of real-estate prices
and what-not; and the local city buses, if there
are any, can take too long for a stranger passing
through to figure out, and taxis are too expensive
for bus travelers.

Some of them couldn't even afford decent luggage, as, every now and then, you would get
what the baggage handlers call . . . an "Arkansas
Samsonite," a plastic garbage bag serving as a
suitcase--why does that make me think of Bill
Clinton and WalMart? Still, you wouldn't want
to buy a cheap garbage bag to carry your be-
longings under a bus, or everything you own
could spill out all over. The passengers with nice
big heavy luggage, I noticed, would do well to
take their unruly bags to "Bag Obedience School."

Let's talk about passenger **luggage** for a minute. For the most part the big city bus depots
have a pretty good system for handling all the

big luggage and freight underneath the buses: it's organized by destination and supposed to be loaded in the baggage bins so that drivers and depots down the road can make sense of it. The problem is: since it's a job that's hard on your back, I noticed a lot of the baggage handlers in places like Denver and Albuquerque . . . were Spanish speaking and couldn't read English. So I tended to have fun calling those baggage claim checks . . . "Lottery Tickets." No passenger wants to have trouble finding their luggage; and no driver wants to have trouble with it either: the hard thing for a driver is when you have a guy getting off at 3am in some tiny town half way between two big cities, and his one little bag is buried under all of Chicago, . . . or is it under Minneapolis? My advice to bus passengers: try to travel light, taking the important stuff on board with you, checking something in under the bus only if you have to.

More people want to fly now, at least before '09, and the buses have been pushed somewhat out of the way--though we still could use them to help the small-towns link-up with the bigger ones. Buses are still quite necessary for some of the smaller legs of a trip, like getting groups to and from airports. I wouldn't be surprised to see more small buses in the future zipping in-n-out of the smaller towns, since a lot of those inhabitants can't afford to drive their own cars as much as they used to.

I remember one time, I had a group that missed an airplane in Colorado Springs because of the weather, or whether, and they commandeered me to drive them to Denver real quick to catch another flight. They were real worried they were going to miss that one too, and they kept pressuring me to hurry up. I told them, "Relax, . . . I'm your pilot too." I think that would be real funny: get some of these sex-tuplets to play a prank on a group of people going on a cruise. They see a cab driver; then the bus driver is the same guy; then the pilot is the same guy; then the next bus driver is the same guy; and, when they get to the luxury-liner, guess who the captain is.

Whereas Greyhound guys wear grey and get paid by the hour, we TNM&O guys wore blue and got paid by the mile--whereas Greyhound was like the Army, we felt like the marines. They had automatic MCIs, we had seven-speed stick MCIs, just like Powder River--very few bus drivers are really qualified to drive such an outfit. In a city like Denver or Albuquerque, Greyhound handles east-west, while TNM&O handles north-south. Where I lived, Pueblo, Colorado, though it was a smaller city, it was a cross-roads of many big cities, so many big buses converge there about 2-pm every day. About half the year, you could always tell the bus from Wichita, because it was the one with by-far the most bugs on the wind-shield--not to worry though, because the frequent hail-storms in the region would take care of that.

On a typical line-run, the bus is like a river flowing down the highway--it says the name of the far-off destination up in the front window: DENVER, LOS ANGELES, NEW YORK, EL PASO, BILLINGS, WICHITA, DALLAS, SALT LAKE CITY, MINNEAPOLIS, or dozens of other cities. Then that long bus run is divided up in to roughly eight-hour driving increments, for the regular drivers. These line-haul drivers tend to need to live in big-enough towns where the line segments would stop-n-start: a driver might live in Denver and drive to Albuquerque or Amarillo, go to the company-paid motel for ten hours or so, then drive back the next day. I was stationed out of Pueblo, Colorado, which is quite a cross-roads town really, between Cheyenne, Denver, and Albuquerque, El Paso, or Amarillo and Dallas, and Grand Junction to Wichita. (In fact, a lot of those classic George Strait songs take place on the same roads I drove on hundreds of time: "Amarillo by Mornin'" and "gotta go now, Baby, if I hurry, I can still make Cheyenne." And I always enjoyed driving south and east out of Pueblo watching for another tumbleweed with a love-note attached to it from Katherine Ross in the movie *Conagher*.) Most line-run segments tend to be about three-hundred to five-hundred miles with several quick stops along the way, like Garden City, Dodge City, and Pratt, Kansas (like in Stephen King's *The Stand*).

The big buses always have a PA system, to announce things to the passengers. Whenever you would start a major leg of a run, the driver would get on the microphone in the first few miles and go over the rules, while welcoming the passengers. You might say something like, "Good Evening, my name is So-n-So, and I'll be your driver all the way to Amarillo, Texas." Then I would give them a preview of the breaks along the way, and then I'd finish with the bus rules, "Please remember: No Smoking, No Drinking, and No Loud Music or Conversation. If you need anything, please don't hesitate to come up to the front here and let me know. Thank you." If I had a smaller more-informal group going say north to someplace like Cheyenne or west to Grand Junction, I would keep it simpler: "Please remember: No Kicking, No Scratching, No Biting." Some drivers really get into the PA announcements, kind of like that enthusiastic stage-coach driver in *A Big Hand For the Little Lady*. The last few miles of a leg, this driver would sort of wake everyone up with the arrival announcement: "We'll be landing in Albuquerque in a few minutes, and this bus will be here for one hour for cleaning. I still get stage-fright when I do this, but: If you are continuing on South from here toward El Paso, you'll stay on this same bus, but we need you to dismount for cleaning and until the new driver calls you to re-board. If you are heading East or West out of Albuquerque, you will transfer to a Greyhound Bus on the other side of the Depot--just match the city-names on your ticket to the city names above the door. Please stay seated until we come to a complete stop. And Thanks for riding TNM&O Coaches."

Again, it breaks my heart a little bit, but a lot of passengers complain about the stops along the way--I don't know why they can't **enjoy the trip**. Even with all the stops, our TNM&O Coaches averaged close to 50mph--that's better than Rob Lowe and the big blond guy were doing on US 50 in *The Stand*, which may be where we are headed with this rat-race and over-population. So what! if a driver has to drop a guy off and check for new packages in Shinbone, Nebraska--are the city dwellers the only ones with a right to have access to a bus route?--especially one that's going that way already anyway? City people need to remember where their food comes from: the rural areas, and small towns shouldn't have to dry up just because the city people outnumbered them and voted them out. . . . There's rich oil man in the movie *Comes A Horseman*, and he makes an ignorant comment: "When it come to the needs of the people over the land, I'd have to side with the people anytime"--what he's forgetting there is a fundamental fact: the people live on the land, and everything they need first comes from the land, not from outer space, not even from the cities. Sure, a farmer in the country might need a tractor part from the city, but where did the iron ore for that tractor part come from? and what good is that tractor part if there's no food to be harvested or maybe even no farmer to harvest it?! . . . These are just some of the things a bus driver like me gets to think about while he's working.

Let's talk about **packages** for a minute. Packages can go a few different methods, the two obvious ones being the U.S. Postal Service and United Parcel Service or Federal Express. But there is a third method for shipping packages that goes underappreciated by most people: the bus lines. Whereas, with the Postal Service and UPS or FedEx, unless you pay through the nose, you don't always know what day a package will arrive at its destination, with the bus lines, you can ship things much more spontaneously and know almost the exact minute it will get to the bus stop of your choice. Whole towns have been saved by a bus driver bringing the inoculations for the diphtheria epidemic just in time--hey, maybe we should start our own commemorative bus race, like the Iditarod Sled-Dog Race. . . . Weddings and funerals can be a great success or failure, depending on whether the bus driver remembered to drop off the flowers or tuxedos. When Tiger Woods won the 1997 Master Golf Tournament, who do you think dropped off his new putter just in time?

When UPS drivers went on strike around the turn of the millenium, guess who had to do all their work for them: line-haul bus drivers.

Imagine having a bus-load of people . . . and all
their luggage; then add all the packages UPS
would have had normally--not a lot of fun, especially when you are paid by the mile. There were
times when I thought I might as well trade in my
blue uniform for some brown clothes. Then I
heard UPS and FedEx were going to merge: . . .
"FedUp."

Regular-Route Line-Run Drivers might do the
same thing for ten years. You see the same bus
driver every other day in Greensburg, Kansas, at
7:33am, except for Sundays, when an extra-board
driver fills in. They might go to the same motel
room every other night: on odd nights, it's Vern's
room; even nights, it Jerry's--but, that one night a
week, it belongs to an extra-board driver, and
who knows who that could be? So the problem
is, some regular line-haul drivers get possessive
of their runs and motel rooms probably in a way
they shouldn't. As far as the runs go, the more
drivers do things right, the more a run might stay
the same no matter who's doing it, the same as
with school-bus routes. When it comes to posses-
siveness of motel rooms, it depends on the motel:
some use different rooms each night, and some
use the same room every night--these are the
ones where the main drivers get the idea that the
room is their personal apartment, and they start
arranging it like it's their own home.

One room in Grand Junction, I noticed, never
had a night stand or a lamp by the bed--well,
there was a lamp, but it was always tucked away
in the closet, and I always had to dig it out and
grab a folding chair and set it up so I could read
myself to sleep. This was routine for quite a few
stays, but it was a hassle; . . . and finally one
night, when I found the lamp, it had been muti-

lated, so I couldn't plug it in. I went to the motel's front desk to ask for a replacement lamp,
where they told me the motel was fresh out. I
unplugged a lamp from the lobby and assured
them, "This lamp will do," and the lady nodded
her head. A few days later, the one of the two
regular drivers was furious at me for plugging
another lamp in by the bed: "That room is my
apartment!" he said, to which I answered, "Not
when I'm assigned to sleep in it." I mean, who
ever heard of a motel bed without a night-stand
and lamp? You can't make your sub extra-board
drivers feel unwelcome. And extra-board drivers, going anyplace at any time, sliding seats
much more often, driving as many as four different buses in a given day, to help out regular
drivers, don't have time for that nonsense.

On that particular run, a driver only had eight
hours off before the turn-around, the minimum
required by law--you have to sleep fast. Ten
hours is wiser, but I've seen as many as sixteen
hours layover for a line driver. One time, I was
driving so fast and furious in all different directions, my boss let me get a motel room in the
town I lived in, right across the street from the
bus station, so I wouldn't have to spend time
commuting eight miles each way.

At some of the turn-around points of line-
runs, a driver may keep a bus but need to get it
serviced, meaning fueled and cleaned inside and
out. Civilian people will not know this, but getting a bus serviced after a long grueling day . . .
can be almost intoxicating to a driver. Pulling
into the fuel pumps at Cheyenne, Wyoming's TA
Truck Stop, a driver can finally relax, as three
truck-stop employees swarm the bus. The driver
doesn't even have to get out of his seat, just sit

there and finish up the day's log book . . . as someone else tends to the diesel, someone else washes the windshield, and someone else climbs on board to clean the inside. . . . It was even better in Wichita, where Kincaid Coaches would take over the whole bus for over a half-hour. Let me tell you: when you are a tired driver, napping in a passenger seat, hearing the water splashing on the windows, the squeegee squeaking on the glass, even the brooms and mops clanging under the seats, . . . you can literally feel what the bus is feeling, . . . and it's like getting a full-body massage yourself.

Meanwhile, a line-haul bus may keep rolling twelve-hundred miles-a-day, getting a cursory quick cleaning at some depots, but sometimes going a couple of days without being turned off in those days. Holidays and the weather don't matter much--the schedules keep rolling. I never relished having to chain-up my bus to get over a mountain pass--it could be dangerous not to chain-up, plus a $500 fine. I often wondered what the meaning of life was, slipping and sliding in a Denver blizzard, with no real choice of stopping.

October of 1997, I dodged a big bullet. I happened to be boarding a plane in Denver to see my Mom in Northwest Iowa, the afternoon of a huge new snowstorm--they got the plane de-iced just in time for me to get the heck out of there. For the next few days, there was a three- or four-foot blanket of snow all over the region, not counting the drifts, with bus-loads of people stuck on the highways like thirty-six hours at a time. I'm sure any stuck buses had enough diesel-fuel in their tanks to keep idling all that time, to keep the passengers warm--most of the big trucks do the same thing when they sleep in the winter, and you can witness hundred of them idling at the same time only inches apart at any given big truck stop.

Holidays are especially silly for bus travel. Being an extra-board driver, I would drive a "double" or a "triple" at the last minute--scheduled runs that normally take one bus take two or three during a holiday rush, making everybody miserable--like they don't have a choice in the matter. Holidays are supposed to be the time when people relax and enjoy themselves the most; but "the system" won't let them--only who set up "the system"? At the start of a Holiday, everyone is frantic that they're late to see their relatives; then on the last night, they're all afraid of losing their jobs if they don't make it back to work in time--the rest of the Animal Kingdom doesn't have all these man-made these problems. This is a big reason I reverted back to the more quiet life-style of driving school buses.

So line-haul bus driving can be quite a challenge even when things are routine. But sometimes, it can be down-right dangerous, with unruly passengers. More than a few times did I drop a guy off at the police station. I didn't go out of my way to find confrontation: for instance, if I smelled cigarette smoke coming from the restroom, I might have pretended I didn't notice it, until a bothered passenger would bring it to my attention--then I would have to deal with it. Almost all the Greyhound drivers I ever saw . . . would not let anyone sit in that pair of seats right behind the driver's seat, no matter how many tickets were sold, except for a fellow driver "Cushioning." I used to be more naive about that, as I tended to let anyone having a rough day sit there.

One time, I picked up a bunch of people in the evening in Colorado Springs, on their way to Denver. The Depot Manager told me about a young man who had been "acting funny," and she told me, "If you have any trouble with him, don't be afraid to drop him off." Well, sure enough, when we pulled into the Englewood, Colorado, bus stop, a passenger from the right front seat told me he saw the young man playing three or four what he described as "Arkansas tooth-picks" . . . and daggers. Even though we were less than thirty minutes away from Denver, I announced an official "smoke break," and we quickly called the cops and had the guy removed.

Another time, a Powder River driver had a close call in the middle of Wyoming on I-25 in the middle of the night. A passenger needed to take a piss, but he went up front and told the driver he did not want to use the bus's rest-room--he said he would prefer to have the bus pull over so that he could take his piss. The debate went back and forth a little while, as the driver continued driving 75-mph, until finally the unruly passenger pulled out a gun and took a shot at the driver's head. Well, the bus hit a bump or something at the right instant, and so the bullet just nicked his ear; a nice and confident passenger from the right-front seat jumped up and threw the guy down in the small stairwell, as the driver quickly pulled over. I guess the bad guy either dropped his gun, or the driver and good passenger were able to wrestle it away from him, and they sat on him, possibly upside-down, until the Highway Patrol was called to the scene by cell-phone.

I didn't know that driver personally, but I'm

sure I saw him in Cheyenne or Denver from time to time before his incident. Interestingly enough, about two years later, I got an old man on my bus going from Denver through Cheyenne, and he claimed to be the good passenger who helped wrestle the bad guy. He said he had ridden with Powder River since then and that the driver who'd gotten his ear nicked . . . had finally quit driving. "The poor guy lost his nerve." . . . Another interesting tid-bit: that old man turned out to be from Gascoyne, North Dakota, within about ten miles of where my Mom was born and raised.

Let's slide seats . . . and move on to **Charter Buses**.

On a School Trip, it's fairly obvious you are taking a group of school students and their chaperones to an athletic event or on a field trip-- Point-A . . . to Point-B, and return. But, with the big over-the-road buses, you could be taking any kind of group of people anywhere at anytime and for any reason, business or pleasure. It could be one-bus and one-driver hauling a group of tourists for a day or a month; or it could be multiple buses going more than sixteen-hundred miles-a-day with multiple drivers sliding seats along the way.

Bus companies that do line-runs usually also do charters, like Greyhound, Gray Line, TNM&O, Powder River, Coach USA. But not every charter company does line runs, like Tauk Tours. Some of the other buses you'll see out there are Arrow Stage Lines out of Nebraska, Lewis Brothers out of Salt Lake City, KeeLine, and others. One little bus company that I've always thought has the best look to it: Karst Stage out of Bozeman, Montana, with a big picture of a stage-coach and six-horse team on the side, an ad campaign as fun as Marlboro Cigarettes and Wells Fargo Banks. Most of the charter and line-run companies really have to do things right, if they want to keep drivers--most school districts would do well to learn some of their little secrets that make a big difference in driver morale, being careful to notice what's the same . . . and what's different, . . . so as not to get things twisted around. With the big charter companies, things can happen real spontaneous real fast, and it takes plenty of good planning beforehand to be able to pull it off.

I'll never forget the days immediately after 9/11--our military was making plans and needed our buses to start hauling them all over the country. After President Bush "Declared War," when I wasn't doing line-runs, I waited by the phone a number of days, waiting for the U.S. Military and my supervisor to "Declare Where." And then I came up with the slogan "God Bus America," because the planes had come to such a standstill. I made a number of trips from Fort Carson, Colorado, to Fort Irvin, California. If you don't think heavy sleep can be contagious, try hauling fifty Army personnel at 3-am with each and every one snoring.

One time, I had a bachelor party out of Fort Collins, going to Las Vegas. They paid a huge damage deposit, and our company gave them permission to have booze on the bus the whole trip. My boss was concerned, so he told me to call him about midnight from Vail with a progress report. When I called him, I got all excited and told him this story: "Neil, it's not a bachelor party at all; it's a Bachelorette Party! and they've been making me drive naked since just west of Denver!" "What?!" he exclaimed, with a hint of regret for not taking the assignment himself. Of course, it was a big story, like I've been known to tell, but I always sound so convincing. Actually, it's probably the best group of people I've ever had, for adults: they never crossed the white line by the driver's seat, and they constantly asked me if I needed anything, like a rest break or some food.

What was the worst group I ever had? you ask. A church group in Colorado, just going twenty miles round trip to enjoy pizza. They were extremely distracting in the heavy Colorado Springs traffic, especially the pastor up front with some of the members of choir. When it was time to leave the pizza parlor, they wanted to stay another hour, and I had a heck of a time explaining that the bus couldn't wait, as it was scheduled to head for Wichita by a certain time-- it took my boss on the phone to get it explained to them. You can't always use God as an excuse for your own selfish desires.

And most charter drivers would agree ski-trips are not the most fun for a driver. A lot of the teen-age skiers and snow-boarders can be a bit spoiled and messy. Then the mountain road can be treacherous and icy. Being a ski instructor in exile during my OTR bus years, it was a burr under my saddle to have to take a ski group: they had no idea they were being driven by **THE GREATEST SKI INSTRUCTOR IN THE WEST**, even if I tried to explain it to them up front there--I felt like Charles Bronson's character Graham Dorsey in *From Noon Till 3*. (That reminds me: someday I've got to finish writing that song "Wichita Ski-Man"--"I am a ski-man without a mountain, . . . and I ain't got much snow. . . .") I didn't even think about skiing on those occasional day-trips skiing, because I was there as a driver--when I am skiing, it's all season long or nothing at all.

I hauled a group of German tourists all over the west for two weeks one time. The second day of our trip, they talked me into going through the two-hundred-mile stretch of the Sand Hills of Nebraska, where the population density is the sparsest on the planet, about two people per square mile. When I was checked out by the Port of Entry in Northeast Colorado, I had to call my boss for some bus paperwork they wanted faxed-- more red-tape and another government fee for something. When we hung up the phone, I found out later, my boss got to wondering, "What the heck is he doing there?! Every bus I know of going from Denver to the Black Hills would go north out of Cheyenne." But he didn't worry; he knew I could be on my own for weeks at a time, getting the job done. The group's leader said, "We have lunch in Arthur," to which I replied, "Not unless we have a deer rifle and a good skinning knife." So I talked them into having lunch in Ogallala. Then they made me drive from there over two-hundred-miles non-stop all the way to Badlands State Park of South Dakota--the old road was hilly and a bit curvy, and I thoroughly enjoyed it, but no driver should be expected to go four hours without a stretch break. I'm sure that set the tone for me not letting anything like that happen again . . . with any group.

Their travel agent had promised them their driver would be able to drive ten hours every day for fourteen days--WRONG: to stay with the log-book limit of 70-hours "On Duty" in 8-days, that's an average of just 8.75-hours-a-day. To make matters worse, my boss used me pretty heavy in the days before the two-week trip began, thus limiting my time available for the tour group--a charter driver can get caught between the group, the boss, and the log-book rules. About four days into the trip, we found ourselves in West Yellowstone, Montana, and the group was upset with me for not being available as much as the travel agent had promised. "In fact," I told them, "if we don't slow down a lot for a couple of days, this driver will be required to take a whole 24-hour period off to stay legal." I assure them and my boss that I would park that bus and leave for good if they didn't cease the debate. You've got to realize, I had lived the recent half of my life within a hundred miles north and south of West Yellowstone, in Bozeman ten years, and in Jackson Hole ten years--just walking down the main drag of that little town, chances were strong that I could bump into someone I knew. My boss was pretty nervous when I told him how the group was trying to wrestle with me, because he knew I was right and had tons of DOT and Law Enforcement on my side, not to mention there wasn't a stick-shift bus driver that he knew of to replace me for hundreds of miles around. He apologized, explained things, and sweet-talked them over the phone, and then everything was fine--"Ah So."

When it comes to charters, it always amazed me how most groups had this narrow notion that the driver invariably would subscribe to their own political or religious beliefs. A lot of groups had no idea that you hauled any other type of group than their own; then some groups thought it was the first time you'd ever seen a group like theirs. It's amazing how driving buses in twenty-four states can broaden your horizons, as long as you try to enjoy the journey. The passengers often had no idea how broad a driver's horizons could be, what you see and learn along the way--I'm sure it's made me a better writer.

I guess it gets back to the many of them perceiving the driver as nothing more than just another part of the bus. "If these walls could talk," when it comes to charter buses, the walls can talk--just ask the driver. One cold-n-rainy evening, while waiting for a group watching a Christmas program, I had two US Air Force Academy Cadet wives waiting on my bus with me, about half my age. They got to talking about their sex lives with their new husbands, with me right there in my driver's seat about two seats away. I started to feel like I was being tortured, then finally the program let out, and we had to get back to work.

For a good-sized bus company that does line-haul and charters both, the **logistics** can be tremendous. This is one of the things that was so amazing about my boss Neil Byrne: he could keep track of dozens of buses and twice as many drivers all at the same time, and then he'd even get behind the wheel himself when there was no one else. When he gave me an assignment, that's why I always strove not to bother him with problems I could try to handle myself.

One evening, on the telephone, he asked me, "Do you want to do a Pinon Canyon with me tomorrow?" That's a gig hauling Fort Carson soldiers to or from a place about a hundred-twenty-five miles from Fort Carson. He gave me the spot time, and bus number, and that was that. The next morning, as I was leisurely getting ready for work, I got a funny feeling something wasn't right, so I called him on his cell-phone: "Hey,

Neil, that spot time is as Fort Carson, isn't it?" to which he answered, "No! the pick-up is at Pinon Canyon to take them back to Fort Carson!" So I was about an hour late, but we were able to laugh about it when we waved to each other on I-25.

I loved watching the weather in the wide-open spaces of that southeast quadrant of Colorado. You could get up in the morning, and there would not be a cloud in the sky. Sometime in the morning, you would see a little white speck start to grow somewhere above Pueblo or Colorado Springs or Trinidad. Driving a bus, you could often follow that growing thunderhead . . . or be chased by it. I grew up smack-dab in Tornado Alley and never saw one tornado; but, in my seven years around Pueblo, I witnessed three nice tornados, two within five miles of me . . . and one really beautiful fifteen-minute one about thirty miles away.

One late night, about 1-am in Tornado weather, heading south out of Lamar, toward the Oklahoma panhandle, I had about an hour-n-a-half to go to get to Boise City, Oklahoma. About an hour south of Lamar, the storm hit us hard, and that bus started rocking and rolling and bouncing, and all the passengers asked me if we were going to make it. About as quick as it started, the bus settled down and again, and we just continued driving in heavy rain, enjoying the lightning show. After an hour-n-a-half, a I started looking for the lights of the small town of Boise City, but there were no lights--"Storm must've knocked out the power," we all thought. Then, a half-hour longer, getting worried about where Boise City, Oklahoma, could be, . . . we found ourselves driving back up into Lamar, Colorado. . . . I had a hard time explaining that one to my boss.

No matter whether line-haul or charters, I enjoyed the *VARIETY!* It was difficult though, dealing with so many varieties of different people--I was not usually on their same wavelength. Even with the variety, I often felt like I was driving my life away; so, "By God," I said, "if I am going to do this, I am going to enjoy it." One thing was sure: I always wanted whoever was sitting up front to be someone I could talk to. They have rules about passengers talking to bus drivers while they are driving--it's a kind of no-no,--but I personally felt like I needed the conversation. Let's put a name on it: TWD, Talking While Driving. With a small load, if there was no one close enough up front, I would often stroll down the aisle and ask, "Is there anyone who wants to come up and **'Ride Shotgun'**?" If I had a guy up front who only wanted to sleep, I would sometimes kindly ask him to move back a few seats, partly so he wouldn't put me to sleep. The occasional guy up front awake who didn't want to converse was tricky for me. And remember: a lot of people don't think a driver is capable of talking. Of course, invariably, sometimes I did most of the talking. I would describe how many red-tail hawks sitting on the poles every other mile or so; or, in the Sand Hills of Nebraska, I noticed a pair of mourning doves every half mile--you could calibrate your odometer by it. Riding on buses occasionally, to get to or from a trip--they call it "cushioning,"--I noticed a lot of Greyhound drivers couldn't talk and drive at the same time, or they might have been just following the rules.

It's true, drivers are supposed to pay attention to their bus's gauges and mirrors constantly, to avoid trouble, and some drivers are better at it than others. Even with all my talking and what-not, I was always able to pull over when circum-stances needed me to. I saved a couple of buses from any extra damage when they suffered flat tires; and I saved a bus or two from having their engines blown when they sprung a major oil-leak or coolant leak. Of course, when the going got tough in heavy traffic, I would shut up and con-centrate intently on the task at hand; but, more often than not, when you travel twenty-four states, mostly west of the Mississippi River, most of the driving can be fairly relaxed, and "TWD," Talking While Driving, sure makes the day or night pass more easily.

I got the same cute little old lady in a group on my bus a couple times a year for a few years who would sit up front, **"Riding Shotgun."** Fi-nally, I realized, "Ma'am, every time I see you, I always end up asking you the same old ques-tions, and you always give me the same old an-swers. Why don't you give me some surprise an-swers for a change?" She laughed and shrugged her shoulders.

Those mobs of old people could be tricky to handle sometimes, swarming the bus before you come to a complete stop, not giving you room to open the air-operated high-powered door. The way they would talk to you about the weather on their way to a casino or some other indoor func-tion, you would have thought they were going on a white-water raft trip. They would often com-pare you to a regular driver the used to see all the time, a driver who spoiled them in every way--and I would have to tell them "I'm not your mother." Sometimes a little old lady would still be in playing the nickel slots fifteen minutes after leave time, getting the whole group riled. The old folks are tricky, but you have to be gentle with them too--just mentioning the possibility of going over some windy mountain road could make some of them bus-sick. Still, you have to know when to be firm: occasionally this 40-year-old man would scold an 80-year-old lady for her discourteous or dangerous behavior: "And, when you get older," I would add, "you'll appreciate why I'm so strict." One time, going through the cafeteria at the Painted Desert of some place, where the bus driver gets complimentary meal, the cashier tells me, "Oh, so you're the driver?--that gentleman over there said he is." They can be sneakier than your average middle-school or junior-high customer. . . . They love their bus trips, those old folks, and they like a fun driver probably more than a safe driver. One old man I saw . . . rode the buses so often, . . . when he stood and walked, his whole slumped posture was still the same as a reclined bus seat.

Don't get me wrong: I have nothing against old folks. It's just hard to be on the same wavelength with them when you're half their age and feel like your life ain't even gotten started yet. Sedentary old folks on long bus rides don't keep you quite as young as teaching skiing, that's for sure. Sometimes I got nervous that one of them might have a heart attack while in my custody; but, looking back, I was probably the one on the verge of having a heart attack. I got a lot of gray hairs hauling the old folks--I think they enjoyed watching me age so quickly.

The thing that did bother me about hauling old folks of that short period: being old doesn't make you right, . . . and it doesn't necessarily make you smarter or wiser than someone younger than you--and I try to keep this in mind myself when hauling high-school kids with big plans and big dreams for the coming big world. It's the old cliche, that "Practice makes perfect"--no it don't: "Only perfect practice makes perfect." In the late 1990s and before 9/11 happened in '01, I think old folks in this country were spoiled: they might have been a kid during the Great Depression--big deal, since they got to learn some valuable important lessons kids of today never got the opportunity to learn, while clicking on their computers and text-messaging,--and they might have suffered through World War II, but they also had the camaraderie of WWII, with the Glory of D-Day, the White Cliffs of Dover, the Big Band Era (much bigger and better than the WWI crowd's "Paddlin' Madelin Home"), and so on, and maybe the Korean War; . . . they got an easy head start economically, in the late '40s or all through the '50s, when everything cost one-tenth or one-twentieth of what it does today; they have no idea what crap the Viet Nam vet went through and may be still going through (even if their '60s music was great); they "invested" and leveraged their money in the out-of-control stock market, instead of in their kids or grand-kids, with not a care of the far-reaching consequences to come. Even the baby-boomers just a hair older than me--when I see that bumper sticker that laughs "We're spending our kids' inheritance," I never have thought that's the least bit funny. It's a question of economic leverage and slavery, and I often resented it when they didn't think once that I might have better things to do than drive my life away, so that they could be retired. The old folks who had spent their life getting out of shape, eating the wrong foods, not getting any exercise, kissing ass and jumping through hoops, and expecting you to do the same--I didn't have much sympathy for them. But the occasional old man who was crippled from ranch work or being a great bronc rider fifty years earlier--these were the few I really loved and respected, . . . and I noticed these quiet guys weren't near as demanding or persnickety about being three inches too far away from the curb. This is why I believe so much more in school buses and young people . . . and the respect and balanced lives school-bus drivers deserve.

When the cogs in your brain turn more than the wheels on the bus, like mine do, you start to understand problem things . . . like wife-beating . . . or police brutality . . . or people "going Postal" at their work place. An awful lot of people's lives are out of balance, . . . and some people in the media--I won't mention any names--thrive on it. Where it comes from, these bad things, is what we need to figure out, so that we can prevent it in the future; or at least people need a way to safely vent their frustrations, without feeling trapped. That's what this book is about: Understanding. There were times when I felt like I was being swept away by a raging current, driving the big buses, or being driven by the big buses--I'm sure there a millions upon millions of other people who feel that way now, even in other businesses. I only hope that . . . future bus drivers and passengers can benefit from what all I have observed and thought about.

My great boss Neil Byrne confided in me one night: "Gary, this Bus Business is the most stressful job I've ever had--and I was a Police Officer! in Colorado Springs!"

. . . So, . . . still, no matter what type of group I had, we generally tried to make the best of it . . . and I tried to appreciate and enjoy each group's company.

Hauling a college basketball team to Hays City, Kansas, I asked them if they wanted to get out on the nearby rail-road tracks . . . to practice their dribbling on the ties: "The court we're going to might have some uneven boards," I said.

"No Extra Charge!" I would often say, referring to my free advice . . . or if something about the trip didn't turn out they way they had planned.

Fed-up with the way our greedy country was going one time, I had an Amish couple sitting up front who I enjoyed asking, "Does one have to be born Amish? or can a guy like me join up? How do I join?" They were flattered by my asking, but I believe they might have thought twice about letting me join.

Being an "on-sabbatical" dude wrangler and ski instructor, I always enjoyed going across Kansas. I would kid people about the Ford Dealership in Dodge, the Dodge Dealership in Ford, and the Chevy Dealership in Fort Dodge. One time, driving a line-run across Kansas, on the way to Wichita, I picked up an old man in his 80s: . . . naturally I asked him if he ever knew Wyatt Earp--he lived until 1929, you know,--and the old man smiled and didn't disappoint me: "Yes," he said, "and you remind me of him a little bit."

Not one to go totally by the book with the big buses, I often wore a Stetson "Open Road" in my travels--you know, the same classic hat that's been worn by many famous characters: LBJ, Harry Truman, Jackie Gleason in *Smokey and the*

Bandit, Harry Morgan in *The Flim-Flam Man,* Chad Everett playing the rich old guy in the remake of *Psycho.* It was not officially part of the uniform, but it sure looked official, and more natural than the Nazi-Germany Gestapo-looking hat some guys wore; I mean, what better hat for an over-the-road bus driver . . . than a Stetson "Open Road"?! You have to reach a certain age and level of maturity . . . to look good in a hat like that. I wasn't always in love with having to wear a uniform, but my "official-looking" unofficial hat really rounded it off.

And I noticed the clip-on tie came in handy for lots of things. Some drivers used it to help check the oil dip-stick; some used it to wipe a smudge off a mirror; some just used it for their own personal napkin. Some drivers used their clip-on tie for all three, which may explain why I occasionally found . . . lip-stick on the dip-stick, grease on some drivers' lips, and runny-egg on some mirrors.

I even had my summer-time uniform shirts specially tailored, not unlike the way Shelley Long finagled her girl-scout uniform in *Troop Beverly Hills*: I didn't like the short-sleeves, so I took some long-sleeve shirts and had them made into half-sleeve shirts--most knew something was different, but they couldn't put their finger on it. When I garage-sailed all my shirts off to fellow drivers, I advertised them as "only driven on Sundays" . . . and "by a slow driver"--some of my shirts even sold for more than they cost new. . . . I noticed a Greyhound driver selling some old uniforms on the bulletin board in Denver one time: his name, believe it or not, was "Willie Taylor"--I think he will.

It was a lot of fun for me to imagine things

while driving. Oh, what the heck, we might as well put a label on this also: *IWD, Imagination While Driving.* I used to tell people kind of a Twilight Zone story about how I got my first bus-driving job: I was working on a ranch, driving an old pick-up and big horse trailer on a country road, when a school-bus pulls up beside me with a bunch of screaming kids. The distraught school-bus driver yells out the window, "Hey, Mister, you wanna trade?!" Tired of the hard work and low pay, I says, "Okay," and we switch lives. . . . Along those same lines, I would ask people along my bus travels the same question . . . if they'd like to switch. "I wonder if that guy would trade me," I would say to the passengers up front. My bus for their vintage Studebaker, my bus for their restored antique farm tractor, my bus for their Harley-Davidson Motorcycle and strong position in the Hell's Angels--"But you have to take the passengers," I was always sure to add, so I didn't have any takers.

I always enjoyed pulling into Dodge City, Kansas, on my way subbing to and from Wichita. I would get on the radio and tell the passenger: "We'll be here twenty minutes, before we get out of town." Both the east-bound and the west-bound buses would break there at exactly the same time, so I always had to warn the people, "Be sure you get back on the right bus, . . . the one with the good-looking driver." Then, visiting with the other driver there, I would always re-mind him, "This town ain't big enough for both of us."

Fairly often, on the line-runs, maybe because I can be so goofy, a passenger would ask, "Are you the driver?" and I would reply, "Naw, I'm an ac-tor learning a part for a new movie about a bus driver." You'd be surprised how many people actually believed me, including me.

You don't know how hard it was for me some-times, to know you've got more talent than Sein-feld or Tim Allen or Jeff Foxworthy, even funnier than some of those Sunday-morning tele-evan-gelists--and there you are driving buses 10,000-miles some months. I had a guy one time on the way through Gunnison--he was on his way to Crested Butte--tell me I'm funnier than Letter-man, as if I didn't already know. It was not un-common for me to get standing ovations at some of the major depots I pulled into, and standing at the door shaking hands with the passengers . . . made me feel like a revered preacher after a pow-erful Sunday-Morning sermon. Still, you'd be amazed how many people don't know you're that funny if you can't show them the proof of being rich and famous for it.

One particularly disturbing time for me was when fel-low driver Larry Leeper showed me a book he'd just read, *The Horse Whisperer*. The Robert Redford movie was re-leased about the same time, so I went to see it at Pueblo's new theater. You can't imagine how discouraged I felt when I witnessed all my *Heinsian WESTERN DANCE* phi-losophy come to life on the big screen. (For those of you who have taken my dance lessons or read my dance man-ual, *HAVE HARMONY WITH WOMEN*, you know what I am talking about.) Since the early 1980s, I have been teaching dancing based on fine horse-training methods, namely those similar to Ray Hunt, and some of His Disciples like Buck Brannaman and Pat Parelli. Since then, I have talked constantly of "sacking the woman out" like a horse, "get-ting her used to things," and "gaining trust," and hence having no resistance bringing out her natural dance abili-ties. Now, in the movie, Redford plays a character who's pretty much an in-between compilation of a younger Bran-naman and an older Hunt. When I saw Redford putting her foot in the stirrup, then when I saw his hand on the small of her back on the Saturday Night dance floor, I realized: that's the "sacking-out" I've been teaching all these years. So the character was a compilation of three men--guess who the third one is. Then, the icing on the cake was when I noticed an extraordinary "coincidence"--that the dance scene was filmed in a country dance pavilion fifteen miles north of Bozeman, Montana, where yours truly gave more than a dozen-week series of lessons a few years earlier--the odds were a million-to-one that the dance scene would be set where I had taught, . . . or were they?

And there I was driving my life away. . . . Remember, in the end of *The Horse Whisperer*, how she decides to go back to her husband? but it's up in the air how that will work out--well, I got the sequel worked out real quick: she goes back to her husband . . . with the stipulation that they take dance lessons together . . . from a guy like me she's heard of out west, . . . so they take the fine dance lessons, . . . and she falls for the dance teacher. . . . No, I'm not crying plagiarism; I'm just demanding respect. I've seen some sort of signature dance moves I teach . . . in TV commercials over the years also, for Aleve Pain Reliever and I forget what else--I believe these commercials are made by people I taught. And these same people were involved or at least associated with Redford's lucrative movie project-- how else would all three parties be associated with the same one-in-a-million dance pavilion?

I think the thing that kept me going all that time was the faith knowing that . . . one day all my books would really come out, and all the hard miles would add up to more fine writing to share with millions more people. And, instead of me just taking credit, credit would be given where credit is due. A little bit of Attribution goes a long way.

Here's an interesting note. There are many more drivers out there with bigger problems than mine, and they might not see light at the end of the tunnel like I always did. Kindly treat them well.

Well, we're not there yet, so let's press on. . . .

One time, after a Major-League Baseball game, a woman asked me if I got to see the game--they let charter-bus drivers in for free, you know. I asked her: "Did you notice the Umpire behind home-plate?--that was me." Our TNM&O uniforms were a similar light-blue shirt and navy-blue pants as the umpires wore, so I think this lady believed me. "They let bus drivers in for free," I explained, "so they try to put us to work inside the stadium."

One Major-League game I drove for, the home team got clobbered something like twelve-to-nothing. I got on the PA system and said, "Unbereavable." It might have been funnier if the tour group had been Chinese.

I knew one driver who shuttled pro NFL Football Teams and pro NBA Basketball Teams to and from the airport quite often. He told me some of the coaches used to cry on his shoulder asking for advice on what to do with some of their misbehaving celebrity players.

I had a lady one time for a hundred miles asking me how to handle her spoiled 18-year-old son. "Ma'am," I said, "there's no getting around it: you're gonna have to wean him--and the sooner, the better." Most of the bus agreed with my professional opinion; and, when she reached her destination, she was confident she had a new resolve.

One time, on a charter to a dinner theater in Denver or Boulder, the group met me at the bus after the play, and a beautiful lady in a nice evening gown asked me: "Oh, what a wonderful evening! Did you get to see the play? Did you get to have a nice dinner?" Of course, I couldn't resist telling her the truth: "The main actor got sick at the last minute--guess who they asked to fill in for him."

Driving the line-haul scheduled runs, I can't tell you how many times people have met on the bus on one side of the country, and then they decide to get married, and sometimes divorced, by the time they get to the other side of the country--it's not uncommon for a bus driver along the way to be asked to be Best Man, especially one as personable as yours truly. Dropping off those packages in a small town in the middle of the night with body parts for someone's surgery--don't be surprised if the local doctor needs to enlist the help of the bus driver for a few minutes, to hold a patient down, hand him a scalpel, or whatever. And talk about delivering babies in the back of a bus: I can't remember how many I have delivered--the Allman Brothers might have a song about it. I already mentioned Tiger Woods's '97 putter, the flowers and tuxedos for weddings and funeral we could easily forget to drop off, and the medicine that can stop a pandemic . . . as long as the bus driver remembers. I'm telling you: the whole country would fall flat on its face if it weren't for all the great bus drivers.

Some of the easiest times I ever had driving big over-the-road buses were while **"Dead-Heading"**--where you drive long distances by yourself . . . empty. There are lots of times when you get a group of people where they need to go, and then the bus needs to get back home again, . . . or you might dead-head to go pick-up a group. In the year 2000, I drove an empty Greyhound Bus from Denver to Los Angeles to be used for the Democratic National Convention.

Dead-Heading a bus is the closest we bus drivers get to feel like a normal Truck Driver. . . With all due respect, OTR semi-tractor-trailer drivers have it easy compared to OTR bus drivers: not that they don't have it difficult enough, with their tough schedules, their bosses, and their fellow drivers; but, take away the passengers, . . . and suddenly you are looking at a much freer driver, free to take charge of their own day, their own breaks, free to pick their favorite CDs to listen to, free to smoke if they want, free to eat when they want, and more free to sleep when they please, as they have their own sleeper berth behind the tractor cab. Talk to some OTR truck drivers at the Interstate Highway Truck Stops, and most will adamantly tell you . . . they wouldn't touch a bus-load-ful of passengers . . . with a ten-foot pole. In fact, many truck drivers might see the bus drivers . . . as fools. Keep in mind, OTR truck driver and OTR bus drivers have the same Log Books to fill out every day, so they have the follow the same laws governing their safe work limits--only bus drivers constantly have that nagging passenger-element hanging over their head even while they are off-duty and sleeping. So Dead-Heading to me was always a treat.

Oh, I should mention **"Cushioning"** here real quick, where a driver rides a bus to get where they need him . . . or to get home again from a long drive. I loved Cushioning maybe even more than Dead-Heading, because you get half pay for it, and you can Cushion a lot more hours in a day than you can drive. If I was tired enough, I would sleep, especially at night, or I might read with the tiny reading lamp; but I always enjoyed **Riding Shotgun.** Some of my longest cushions: from Los Angeles to Pueblo, Colorado, from Portland, Oregon to Pueblo, from Pueblo to north of Grand Forks, North Dakota. A lot of bus drivers hate cushioning, but I loved it: you have to know how to do it in a way, getting cleaned up along the way, and having a good book to read, or appreciating the endless scenery, and having one of those inflatable U-shaped neck pillows really helps. Watch your baggage though--even your own bus company could lose it for a few days. One of the common courtesies among bus companies is: they always haul each other's drivers for free when it comes to cushioning. In my six-year stint with TNM&O, I always enjoyed stepping up to another driver's door and asking, "Is this the *3:10 to Yuma*?" In fact, I could probably put on some bus-driver-looking clothes right now, grab my little brief-case and a small travel bag, and go to any interstate bus-stop in the country, . . . and tell any driver I please . . . that "I'm cushioning"--I might have to make up some story about the trip I'm coming from or the trip I'm headed to-- . . . and he would probably have me sitting in the seat right behind him pronto. I've always love the idea of "throwing cushion to the wind." The trouble is, I can't think of anywhere I want to go right now without having my own wheels there when I get there.

Once every fall, my company would cushion several drivers to Pembina, North Dakota, touching the Minnesota and Canadian borders, where MCI (Motor Coach Incorporated) Buses are made. Then we would dead-head the new buses down to Lubbock, Texas, the corporate headquarters. That was always enjoyable, as long as the other drivers didn't try to make a race out of it. One group the week before me one year made the trip in 42-hours, setting a new record, or standard; when I came along with five buses a week later in a slower pace of 48-hours, the Safety Director asked me what took us so long-- everyone including the other four drivers blame me for slowing them up. "We got a quick tour of the factory, drove the speed limit, and didn't cheat on my sleep or my log-book," I told him. "Oh," he said. "No extra charge anyhow," I reminded him, "since we get paid by the mile." Not only that, but, of the five of us, they had sent me, the only Colorado driver, a day to soon--so I had to twiddle my thumbs laid-over in Grand Forks and extra twenty-four hours. And we had gotten lost in Wichita for two hours, because one of his Texas drivers up front . . . failed to follow the simple etiquette of keeping the bus behind him in his rear-view mirror--we got split up, and no one knew who was too far ahead or too far behind.

The arrival at the destination is fine, but it always gets back to **enjoying the trip** for me--it has everything to do with morale and safety. It's important to enjoy the job; otherwise how can you do it?

There's a kind of **Etiquette** out on the open road, or some **Camaraderie** among the professionals . . . that makes the job more enjoyable. Cars often don't know anything about this, but, if you start watching the big rigs, the semi-tractor-trailers . . . and the big buses, mostly on the Interstate Highways, you'll notice them communicating with each other, mostly with their lights, in the day-time as well but mostly at night. When one rig passes another, the rig that just got passed will turn-off his head-lights for a second or two, as a courtesy to let the passing rig know there is enough room to return to the right lane. When two rigs that may know each other meet, going opposite directions, they will flash their left-turn signals to say hello. One TNM&O driver, I remember, would go hog wild with this one: he would flash everything on-n-off, his head-lights, his clearance and marker lights, the destination sign, as well as his turn-signal, much like a Los Angeles DJ. I never knew which driver it was, until one night I was cushioning in the back of his bus, and my reading light would go off-n-on a couple of times--coincidentally, I noticed out the left window there was another TNM&O bus on the other side of the Interstate. Unfortunately, some of the fancy technology on the newer equipment won't let drivers turn off their head-lights whenever they please, taking some of the human element out of over-the-driving. Some hard-core authorities talk about this turn-signal greeting being a safety hazard, but I don't think it is: drivers don't do it in heavy traffic, they reserve it for the open road, where at 3-in-the-morning in Northeastern New Mexico, it can feel like two ships passing in the night in the middle of the Pacific Ocean.

Regular-route drivers, with same routine every other day, meet other drivers on the road and wave to them about the same time every day and on the same spot in the road. A regular driver will often see the same bus route going the opposite way, or you might see a UPS truck, or it could be a furniture delivery truck, or an auto-parts truck. The regular drivers kind of get to know each other's routines, but the closest they ever get is a friendly wave every other day. When I subbed for all those regular drivers with TNM&O, I noticed these other regulars from the other businesses, and so I knew the guy I was subbing for would want me to wave back--a sub not paying attention would not be ready to wave, and this can upset the rhythm-of-the-road somewhat. Each driver has a certain kind of wave--it's like a signature; so a sub is not going to have the same wave as a regular driver. A regular driver can tell a sub in the other rig right off the bat, because the wave will be out-of-kilter--Heaven forbid a driver would steal another driver's wave. But I got to thinking: I wonder how many subs are waving back at subs thinking they're waving at back at regular drivers.

When you spend a lot of time out on the open road, you start noticing the idiosyncrasies of each big company. A lot of companies would have their buses governed at a certain speed in the name of safety. Our TNM&O Coaches were generally governed at 72-mph; Swift Trucking and JB Hunt were governed at a slow 65-mph--this is useful information when it comes to blending in with the traffic. I wish the civilians in the cars knew about big-rigs being governed: they get too upset when they are behind a 72-mph rig trying to pass another rig governed at 70-mph--there's no understanding there, just road-rage. Still sometimes you might acquire a bus where you could over-ride the governor.

One time, I got a spur-of-the-moment call on my red phone to rescue a group of high-school baseball players in Farmington, New Mexico-- they needed to catch a plane in Colorado Springs the next morning, and every minute counted. Whenever I talked to my boss, I always called him "Governor" as he gave me my assignments and instructions. Luckily, I got old Bus #913, and it could do 80. When I got to the group about 2:30-am, they questioned whether I could make it back in time. A half-hour out on the road, and they were all sleeping like a baby, not worried. Also, luckily, the road US 160 was wide open compared to other US highways, and there was a full moon. I don't normally condone speeding, but this time it felt right going a little over, with good light and no one else on the road, so I got them there with an hour to spare. My boss was shocked and kind of pleased that "the dawdler" saved the day. One thing I notice about smooth driving: I truly believe . . . that my strong expert skiing skills have made me a better driver--I can feel the road the same way a good skier feels the snow and terrain as it comes, and that's what makes things smooth.

There is an unwritten rule out there that generally says each driver won't tell the others how to drive. Sometimes a professional bus driver will find himself hauling a half-dozen or so other drivers somewhere--and then you become the Drivers' Driver. The camaraderie can be kind of nice then.

But each driver tends to have his quirks. One older driver, after thirty years, still couldn't shift worth a darn, grinding all the time--I think he was just getting too worn-out, and so everyone let him be. One driver, named Woody, I would always greet with "Would he? or wouldn't he?--I think he would." Another driver named Dewey, I would greet with "Do we? or don't we?--I think we do." You'll notice a lot of the older drivers are in pretty poor physical condition, barely able to pass the DOT Physical. But a few of the younger and middle-aged drivers stay in excellent shape, if they stay on top of it.

One younger driver out of Albuquerque had some amazing driving skills. I've forgotten his name, but he was a big black guy that looked more like a pro football player than he did a bus driver. He could drive the seven-speed sticks like a race-car; and, if you gave him a 103-inch hole, in heavy fast-moving traffic, he could slip our 102-inch-wide buses through it before the other motorists knew what happened. I rode with him from time to time south out of Denver in the evenings to get back to Pueblo--I always found it very entertaining. But, one day, I heard he got a wreckless-driving ticket pulling out of Denver--I thought that was pretty funny: a bus driver in a big bus getting a wreckless driving ticket. In a way, I was proud of him though: he had the skills to drive in NASCAR or at Indy, yet he subjugated his ego low enough . . . to drive a common bus day-in-n-day-out--I doubt Jeff Gordon or Dale Earnhardt could do that.

That's some of my fonder memories of driving the big buses. Unfortunately, there are some not-so-fonder.

Besides hitting a number of birds on the wind-shield . . . and a few varmints on the road, I only hit one deer in my career, and it was going a slow 35-mph on a wide road down a mountain pass, which is pretty ironic, but it bothered me. Once in awhile, if you had a bus with the air-condi-tioner not working, we would have to open the roof vents, and I would warn the passengers about the exciting possibility of a red-tail hawk flying in.

One driver, we noticed, was hitting more elk on the Interstate than was probably his fair share. He was a night driver out of Albuquerque; and, over time, I noticed he would set his cruise con-trol and cross his legs while driving through the night--I'm sure that slowed his reaction time. Another driver did the same silly thing, setting the cruise and crossing his legs, only he did it not too far north of Denver, which wasn't too bright, and he did rear-end somebody one day to prove his slow-reaction time. That driver eventually took my great boss's place, because of health reasons that curtailed his driving, and because they couldn't find anyone else to take the stressful job. While everyone generally keeps theirs mouths shut about other drivers' flaws, it's hard to take orders from someone like that.

It's a sad fact: there is **some ugliness** out there. One time, a fellow driver told that he had hit a dog, . . . and he said he had to put it out of its misery--the hard way--in front of the passengers. Another time, stuck in city traffic, my whole bus saw a pigeon that was crippled and flopping around on the pavement, the motorists helpless to euthanise the poor bird. There ought to be more retention of common sense in the world, more empowerment of the people to do what needs to be done naturally, instead of everyone playing the victim.

I saw way too many bad accidents in my six years over-the-road, not witnessing the accidents as they happened necessarily, thank God, but seeing the aftermath a short time later with the Highway Patrol or someone calling-them already on the scene--cars upside down, and fatalities, and ambulances, and clean-up crews. . . . Being a spontaneous extra-board driver, going any place at any time on a moment's notice, there were countless times when I was "behind schedule"--I've often wondered how many of those bad accidents I might have been in . . . if I had been "on time."

One driver, a friend of mine, a regular-rout driver, had his share of first-hand bad luck with bad accidents. He rear-ended a family in a car one time, and that was pretty bad for the family. About a year later, he ran over a pedestrian on a Denver street and killed him. He was often regarded as one of our better drivers, but I noticed he could have slowed down a bit and kept himself more of a space-cushion.

One driver I knew . . . had a head-on collision with a small car that came into his lane, an apparent suicide. The bus driver and passengers survived all right, physically, I guess. The bus was able to be repaired and put back into the fleet, but I'm not sure about the driver's nerve.

Most of the OTR drivers I have known were all quite-confident very-assertive people, as you really have to learn to watch out for yourself and stick up for yourself, among thousands of other drivers you rub bumpers with, the millions of passengers you rub elbows with, and a few higher-ups you occasionally see face-to-face. I never felt guilty for being known as "the dawdler."

One time, I had the high-ranking executive Safety Director bragging to me about how he could drive his car . . . from Lubbock . . . to Denver . . . non-stop, implying that I should be able to do the same. I reminded him that that wasn't even close to being legal, especially not with a bus, and I told him to "BACK OFF!" . . . I further got back at him at the Christmas Party one year, when he was trying to remember the name of the fancy Mexican restaurant he takes all the new drivers to: when no one could help him remember the name after several seconds, I blurted out, "Taco Bell?" to which a couple of drivers burst out laughing--and that was probably another instant that marked the beginning of the end for me.

Yes, sometimes drivers can be a bit cruel to each other, with different silly factions, or feelings of superiority, and so on.

One group of Texas drivers, sliding seats with

Colorado drivers at the Lamar Truck Stop, . . . would pull in nose-first perpendicular to the restaurant . . . for the next driver to have to: put the bus in reverse, watch out for little cars coming and going for the restaurant and the gas pumps, and watch out for pedestrians. On the surface, it doesn't look like anything's wrong, but, on closer inspection, it's actually an animalistic territoriality-n-aggression thing from one group of drivers toward another. Common sense and courtesy tells a good driver to parallel park a bus out away from the congestion, so the next driver can just climb in and drive forward, which is much easier and safer for everyone.

That same group had a driver meeting me to switch buses in Boise City, Oklahoma, one day, and experience and knowledge of the runs told everyone we would probably arrive there at precisely the same time. Well, at our Springfield, Colorado, bus-stop, one of his cohorts talked me in to meeting him fifteen miles north of Boise City instead, at a small picnic spot by the Cimarron River--you can see it on a map. Well, we got there, . . . and my passengers had to wait almost thirty minutes, in 100-degree heat with no food or facilities, . . . for that other driver to show up and trade me routes. Well, again, it doesn't look like any big deal, but here's what motivated him: he got thirty more miles that way, while the Colorado driver got thirty less--that's a difference of over $20 in pay between the two. And: the bus he brought me didn't lose any time in the schedule, while the bus I brought him . . . became over a half-hour late. Childish.

Speaking of making other members of the human species back-up. When I became the school-bus driver of the pre-school I mentioned earlier, a former driver found out a month into my job . . . that I had a couple of stops where I routinely backed my bus out of driveways. She challenged me about my routine backing, citing that the backing-up of school-buses can be highly danger-ous and is very-much frowned upon and in some cases illegal. Well, when the higher-ups got in-volved, they realized that Uncle Gary only backs up when he absolutely has to, that, in these rou-tine back-ups: the parents knew their role, the monitor knew her role, and all kids were always accounted for. Again, it was nothing more than a case of one aggressive human-being trying to make another human being turn submissive, just like the rest of the animal kingdom--you can see it in horses, coyotes, wolves, and many other species

I don't know these other drivers I'm describ-ing here even knew what they were doing--they were just acting natural. But me, being the writer I am, nothing gets by me, and you have to get up pretty early in the morning if you are going to try to put one over on me. I don't mean to spend my life going around finding fault with other driv-ers; I want to be on every driver's side; but, when they try to find fault after fault after fault with me, I will stand my ground and keep them honest every time. Even when people do "good" things, I like to lay their motives bare . . . and find out what they are really up to--that even goes for some of our most major religions.

We need to talk about **Staying AWAKE** for a minute here--no, for quite a hours, day-after-day, week-after-week, month-after-month, year-after-year. I don't know a professional driver alive who hasn't had to battle with trying to keep his

eyes open from time to time. Falling asleep at
the wheel is a fact of life out on the open road,
even when you think you've gotten enough rest.
A good driver will know this and understand it,
and he will have a plan to handle it so it never
happens to him--this will keep his bus-load safe
and probably some innocent vehicles around him.

Coffee is an obvious possibility, and so is a
caffeinated soft-drink; but these aren't necessarily sure-fire tactics. Talking with someone up
front is one of the surest things for me--this is a
big reason why I'm such a proponent of it. Anyhow, my wheels are always turning, not just on
the bus, but in my mind. You can pass all the
laws you want to against passengers talking to
the driver; but I am going to talk while I'm driving before I fall asleep and kill everybody. If
talking isn't available, chewing gum does won-
ders for me--passengers would often witness me
putting a fresh stick in my mouth when the going
got tough. Another driver told me his preference
was chewing on ice: I remember cushioning into
Pueblo with him at dawn one time up from Albu-
querque--man, you should have seen him grabbing that ice out of the cup, swerving and grabbing, swerving and grabbing, . . . while the rest
of the bus slept, but we made it. Then another
obvious one is . . . sunflower seeds--they almost
always work, but you need a bottle of Diet Coke
to go with them. . . . And, if none of that works,
you had better pull over for a break, . . . no matter what the schedule.

The worst I ever had it sleepy-wise was one
time in the middle of the night hauling the U.S.
Military to Fort Irwin, California: it was between
3- and 4-am, and I had to pull over once every
twenty minutes about four times in a row, while

forty-seven soldiers snored. Not one of them knew about any of those breaks, and it taught me how dangerously-contagious sleep can be. Anyhow, anybody who doesn't understand and agree with what I'm talking about here . . . doesn't have much experience . . . and is in denial.

Another recipe for putting a bus driver to sleep: senior citizens playing BINGO on the bus. I used to haul a group from Trinidad, Colorado, to Pojoaque, New Mexico, to the big Indian Casino there--it was over three-hundred miles for me one way, then a five-hour layover, and six-hundred miles round-trip. South of Raton, they would take my PA microphone and pass out all the BINGO cards. The group leader would set up in the seat right behind me, and she'd be turned around facing the group. Her monotone voice calling number after number after number for more than an hour at a time . . . combined with the morning sun beating in the driver window--it was extremely hard to stay awake. When I felt like dozing off, I discovered a new tactic . . . that was more fun than I had ever dreamed. When there would be an extra long time without a BINGO, with half the bus just needing one more number, as you could hear everybody murmuring about it, . . . I would quietly yell "BINGO!" and the group leader would look all around confused, "Who said that? Who's got a BINGO?" while the rest of the bus would groan in agony. Then, when there would be some other false alarm, she would urgently announce, "Don't clear your cards, because we don't have a BINGO yet!" to which I would immediately say, "Oh, darn, I already cleared my card." Remember, most of these old folks are hard of hearing, so they never knew where I was coming from. Whenever she called

"I-25," I would always yell "BINGO!" since that was the road we were traveling on. They would play special games like "postage stamp" and "layer cake," and I would suggest, "Why don't you try playing 'marble cake'?" "B-4" you criticize me, it may have seemed cruel, but my bingo behavior was pretty "B-9" really, and it was a matter of staying awake and not crashing that bus. About an hour after they would be done playing, for old-time's sake, I would take the PA mike and say, "O-71, . . . O-71," and someone on the bus would shout out, "I don't have a card yet, I need a card."

You can't be too careful when trying to stay awake. There are lots of things a driver has to combat in that regard. Certain frequencies of voices or passengers whispering can get you when they are a few rows back and you can't quite make out what they are saying. It's more important to try to understand the dangers and talk about it in order to prevent accidents . . . than to just call a driver "GUILTY!" every time you hear of a driver falling asleep or crashing a bus.

Now I want to talk about a related issue: **Eating While Driving**, or EWD--I am a proponent of it too, and for very good reasons. When you are a professional driver with a lot of ground to cover every day of the week, complete with awkward schedules and long tedious layovers opposite short-n-quick motel rests, . . . you need to learn how to survive. Remember, if you have only eight hours off between two difficult long drives, it doesn't make any sense to have dinner the night before and breakfast as soon as you wake up--that hardly gives a guy any time to shower and sleep. Getting my sleep in those OTR years was always my first priority.

So, if I had to be the first one out of bed for a trip, here's how I always did it: I slept as late as I possibly could, then I met the group with something light like coffee and a muffin right with me, and I might not nibble at the muffin until we got an hour or so down the road, and that was breakfast; then I'd be good to go for a while until the group stopped for a meal; a lot of times I wouldn't be overly hungry at meal-time, so then I would order something to go, and again I wouldn't have to touch it until an hour or so down the road--this way, meal-times for me were a time of relaxation instead of times to get busy eating. It's no fun hopping into the driver's seat right after a Country Buffet Thanksgiving Dinner knowing you've got a few hundred miles to go yet, and a lot of passengers don't understand that. Keep in mind: you don't have to be dangerous about it, as you can choose food that's easy to handle, like peanut butter versus mayonnaise, or a hamburger or burrito versus spaghetti--then again you might know of a five- or ten-minute break down-the-road where you can dig into that difficult plate. And common sense will tell you, even with the easy food, don't be monkeying with it in heavy traffic; there's almost always a big open road ahead, where things are pretty relaxed--and, if you drop a french-fry, just let it drop, and don't try to be a hero. In heavy traffic, sure, pay attention; going down a mountain pass, sure, pay attention. To tell drivers they can't be nibbling on something in the middle of Wyoming or across Nebraska somewhat silly, in my opinion. And certainly on an hour-long school-bus route, your stomach can wait. Just the same, if you're dead-heading and don't have such an urgent schedule, it makes sense to have a nice sit-down meal whenever you can . . . or to stay in bed and extra hour or two.

Just between you and me, most of the professional drivers I know don't have any problem with Eating While Driving, "EWD" as I call it, as long as you are careful. In the olden days, most buses came with places for drivers to put their drinks and food; nowadays, you'd think a driver would be put before a firing squad for touching one sunflower seed. No, in my opinion, nibbling on some food spaced throughout the long day . . . is one of the best ways of keeping a driver interested . . . and helping him stay awake--which is good for safety.

Still the Powers-That-Be will always be able to point out some single accident way back when where the driver nibbling on some food is what caused the accident. I say, for every life lost because of eating-while-driving, millions more for are saved. It's easy for the Powers-That-Be to make new rules: it's a power trip, and most of them don't even drive, and being former drivers doesn't count--it's the ones that are driving now I care about. It's always fun for them to find another way of making the hard worker feel guilty--"We are all Sinners."

No, if you really look into it like I have, too much of the newer fancy technology kills just as many people as anything else. One has only to go back and remember what I wrote about door buttons and things like video-player volume controls. Hunting for the darn electronic controls for the newer-type automatic transmissions is trickier than grabbing a french-fry. The thousands of days I've driven, and the close to a million miles, I don't remember ever having a group complain about my driving, except that I was too slow for some of them--but then, when you're in the back of a forty- or forty-five foot bus, and the driving is smooth, 75-mph can feel like 35, honestly.

A quick word about Cell Phones and Driving. I would agree that there are too many people out there fiddling with their cell phones in traffic, especially the ones dialing and text-messaging while driving. If my cell phone rings while I'm driving, I simply hand it to the nearest passenger or trip leader . . . and ask them to take a message for me, . . . and I can relay a message back through them to the caller--a lot of times, for a trip driver, it's about directions or an arrival time anyway. Remember, almost all bus drivers have a PA system they need to use while driving, and many have two-way radios to stay in contact with the dispatcher or other buses. And I see nothing wrong with using a head-set for a cell-phone on a long drive, as long as you don't do any dialing while driving--heck, jet airliner pilots have head-sets to stay in touch with Air Traffic Control. It's just a matter of "knowing the difference between route and rung."

When I worked with TNM&O Coaches, I always felt sorry for the Greyhound drivers I came in frequent contact with--they were hen-pecked and harassed with more piddly rules, and they were constantly being watched with distrust by all the government agencies and even their own supervisors. I saw one driver get a $400 fine for not quieting down a loud passenger soon enough for a DOT Agent's tastes. That DOT Agent could have identified himself and given the driver a chance, and he could have even helped the driver handle the loud passenger--instead of taking a number of days pay with the stroke of a pen.

Maybe now is as good a time as any to talk about some bus crashes that have been in the news over the years, all of which the driver was probably the first to go, being up front there in the nose of the ship. . . . One crash, a charter bus in Texas, just an hour into the trip, about 9-am, the driver hit the pillars of an underpass at full speed--six or eight people died. The witnesses told of him standing up from his seat and trying to adjust a mirror moments earlier; but maybe he had tried to do it before rolling, and the passengers harassed him for taking too long to "get this show on the road." And maybe he had to drive three hours to reach the group before their trip even began. . . . One crash, a roll-over in Monument Valley, where ten Chinese tourists died, the witnesses reported that the driver had been fiddling with the door switch; but it may have really been the video-volume control, which the passengers would be embarrassed to admit. . . . Another crash, a Texas church group in Colorado heading home from a ski trip, the bus was going downhill too fast just west of Canon City, and he didn't make the curve--six to nine killed. It could be the group was constantly commenting for a week on how slow he was--then, after the tragedy, that interesting tid-bit of information gets lost in the shuffle. . . . Of all these crashes and many others, the driver invariably becomes the scapegoat, the guilty party, which is easy for the survivors, since the dead driver is no longer around to defend himself . . . and especially if they have something they wish to keep a secret. Tragedies all, yes, and we don't even know how many passengers end up crippled for life from these accidents; but I notice on a lot of the body counts: the driver's body is usually not included in the passenger body count, indicating an attitude that he was more like just part of the bus.

So, maybe a lot of our modern-day bus crashes are due to "driver error"--but my question is this: what was *the cause* of the driver error?! I'll bet you, more often than not, it's **too much bus technology, too many bells and whistles**, for the average driver to keep track of easily. Remember, bus drivers are not fighter pilots operating high-tech helicopters and fighter jets-- those fighter pilots crash-n-burn with whole crews just in practice from time to time, even with no enemy shooting back, because of how complicated and on-edge their job is. This is why I think it's stupid for bus drivers to pretend we're the Blue Angels.

And, in any bus crash, you've got to ask the obvious: was the driver cheating on the log book? And, if he was, was it his own idea? or was his boss or coworkers strong-arming him into doing it? There's a lot of drivers out there who have to driver farther faster to keep up with their growing debt, with mortgage payments, car payments, alimony and child support. I noticed in the bus paper-work one time, of two different buses that had been on the same trip together, the two drivers drove over 500-miles from point-A to point-B, . . . then they instantly slid seats and drove each one the other's bus back from point-B to point-A- -that way they could make it look like they were sleeping when they were driving a double shift. --That's extremely dangerous and illegal, and the cheaters get double the pay, while the legal drivers get half the pay.

In my six-year stint OTR, I met a good percentage of older drivers who were retired from a twenty-some-year military or law-enforcement career--"Why are they even working?" I thought, "don't they have a good-size retirement-check or pension coming in?" So that makes the business that much more of a **"route race."** Too many Americans, in my opinion, do not know how to not work.

One driver I drove with quite a bit with on charters, Norm Smart, was still going strong at 72--until he died of a heart attack: doing charters ninety-nine-point-nine-percent of the time, finally one evening he was assigned to double or substitute a line-run out of Colorado Springs. I'm sure that's what killed him, the stress of being assigned a line-run, which can be much tougher duty than a charter with a more festive atmosphere--they found him in the bus in the garage just minutes before departure time. Don't get me wrong: some line-haul guys can't do charters; and it takes a much-more flexible and spontaneous extra-board driver to be able to do both. Anyway, whenever I drove with Norm, I always remembered the movie *Dumb and Dumber*, where Jim Carey and Jeff Daniels are too stupid to get on-board that bus full of babes on some kind of bikini-modeling tour. I told Norm Smart, "They're going to make a movie about me and you someday--*Smart and Smarter*.

Then you've got unscrupulous bus companies that break all the major common-sense safety rules. One company named Tourismo Rapidos, whizzing up and down I-25 between El Paso and Denver around the turn of the millenium, got caught using the baggage bins under the bus as a sleeper berth for the drivers--talk about a miserable way to try to rest, and they could have suffocated. I wouldn't doubt it if they were hauling illegal aliens from Mexico. I'm sure my own company hauled them from time to time, without knowing it. I don't mean to sound prejudiced, but there were times when I was the only white-guy on the bus and the only one who could speak English--that can seem a bit uncomfortable for a guy who was born in northwest Iowa in 1958.

I've mentioned my great boss Neil Byrne a number of times. I had fun telling him is name is why it's a good idea to wear knee-pads when playing basketball--otherwise "Knee'll Burn." He's one of the biggest factors I lasted as long as I did going twenty-four states over-the-road for six years. He was about the fourth-highest-ranking guy in the company; and, not only was he a great manager, he drove quite a bit, and he was fun to drive with. When one of the top two men put their 30-year-old son ahead of him, he took it as a slap in the face and resigned--and no one could blame him. That was the beginning of the end for me as well. For the next year, my new supervisor expected me to behave more like a bus than a human--he didn't know how to juggle a couple of dozen drivers coming and going at all hours in several different states. I would get done with a six-hun-dred-mile trip, and the phone would ring again only six hours later, before the euphoria had worn off from the last trip, which is illegal and inhuman.

Finally, I was physically attacked by a fellow driver while laid-over at a motel in Holbrook, Arizona, for not agreeing to "doctor" my log book. I called the Safety Direc-tor in Texas, the third highest guy in the company, and got him out of bed about 1-am Texas time to tell him that one of us two drivers was not finishing the trip--I told him to guess which one. It took him a few minutes, but he figured it out. When I got back from that trip, they had a trumped up "charge" against me, that I didn't play the videos loud enough for the group, which was regular Army, which is hard of hearing and not as gentlemanly as the Marines or

Special Forces--but that wasn't my problem. They couldn't fire me, because I had done nothing wrong, . . . but I noticed that my phone never rang again to do any more assignments.

I ran into fellow driver Jeffery Jones several months later, and he said he was sorry to see me leave the company. "If it will make you feel any better," he said, "since you've been gone, Heins, we've been driving a lot of our multiple-bus moves . . . in the 'Missing-Man' Formation."

That's another one of my pet peeves: video controls. A lot of charter buses started playing video movies by the late 1990s. The controls are right up front there under the driver's jurisdiction, as they should be. But the volume control is especially tricky because it is a digital control that you have to look for with your eyeballs, unlike an old analog knob you could just feel; invariably the group will pester you twenty times during a movie: "Can you turn it up? Can you turn it down? Can you turn it up again?"--because the shoot-'em-up scenes are always loud, and the tender love scenes are always quiet, for marketing purposes, so that you have to watch a movie several times to catch everything. I always tell a group up front, "On a bus, there are two settings, too loud and too quiet. If you want a real movie experience, go to a theater, because a driver can't be hunting for that volume control all the time."

Keep in mind, there are actually two places where you can control the volume--besides the driver's control buttons, there may be another one at the player itself in the overhead compartment above the front passengers. But it's easier for the passengers to make the driver keep track of the volume, although it's dangerous--but, even if they would take control, I would end up turning it down anyway, because a driver has to be able to hear himself think.

And now comes one more pet-peeve: when the movie gets to the end, someone in the group invariably pops up to put an end to that VHS tape or DVD before the credits can roll. Now, if you're a real connoisseur of movies, it's only right to watch the credits roll, to see all the names of the people who created the fine work (of course, if it's a bad movie, you might want to turn it off in the first five minutes); but, even better, especially if you're a driver who can't see the movie, the best music is played the last few minutes while the credits are rolling. Listen to that stuff, like the musical scores at the end of great classics like *Tombstone*, or *Open Range*, or *Gunfight At the OK Corral*--who in their right mind would cut off Frankie Lane? . . . When they make a movie about me, I hope the viewers have more respect--or I'll have to write another book about respecting movie makers. When I make it big, after I've sold enough of these books, I am going to make a movie . . . where the shoot-'em-up scenes are too quiet, and the tender love scenes are too loud.

So you can see, over-the-road buses are a tougher business than people might think. Whether line-runs or charters, it takes a lot of good people to make it all run smoothly and safely, . . . and to keep the best people in the business. It helps if they see each other as people, recognizing each individual's unique qualities, in order to foster a warm and friendly atmosphere. And, in a lot of ways, the bus driver needs to be the most confident person on the bus--like that driver in the movie *Bus Stop* protecting Marilyn Monroe from that rambunctious cowboy. The last thing he needs is low self-esteem and all the undue stress from all the angles covered in this book.

There's one more driver I want to remember: Joe Haley, who drove between Pueblo and Wichita when I knew him. He'd show up at 12-midnight, an hour-and-a-half before his run would start--he was lucky his bus was already parked there at the depot so he could give it a thorough checking over, unless it was late getting back from a charter. I don't believe it was a coincidence that Joe had the run he had, with the kind of logistics he preferred. Some line-segments don't give a guy more than a couple of minutes to do a proper pre-trip inspection; but Joe liked to take close to an hour. He was the most conscientious driver I ever met, and he knew as much about the inner workings of a bus as the mechanics did. He would write paragraphs describing even the slightest flaws--and his handwriting was more elaborate than John Hancock's. He brought a bus back to me one time headed for Grand Junction, and he had written, "Bus slow on hills"--I said, "Joe, there aren't any hills between Pueblo and Wichita." One time, because of a driver getting sick or a bus breaking down, Joe had to drive a bus to the south to the top of Raton Pass in July--I said, "Joe, was it snowing on the pass?" He was a great guy--I'm sure he still is,--and he still may be doing that Wichita run, wondering "I wonder whatever happened to Gary Heins."

In a lot of ways, we were opposites, but I learned a lot from Joe, and we always had fun rendezvousing when we did. I know Joe knew we were opposites too: whereas, as far as I know, he did everything by the book, I tended to shoot from the hip most of the time--but he never harped on me about anything, and I think we both knew, if I weren't there doing the spontaneous stuff, there might not be anyone there to do it. A couple of things we tended to agree on: the newest buses are getting too many bells and whistles to be sensible, the wheel-chair lifts, brought about by the American Disabilities Act, needed to be made a lot simpler. The new maximum-length buses of 45-feet need another axle added, probably in the front, so there are two axles in the front like Army trucks have. Joe Haley, I, and another great driver, John Elliot, all agreed the new automatics are not necessarily safer to drive: they can shift of icy roads when you don't want them to, causing you to spin-out-- the old stick-shifts may be more difficult to drive, but they give a driver more control. I think it's a good idea for school buses to be automatics, because of all the stops and so drivers can monitor the kids a lot easier; but big over-the-road buses tend to alienate a driver when they get too automatic.

Speaking of John Elliot, he rescued me one time from a Mutiny brewing on my charter bus. I was on a week-long trip out in Portland, Oregon, and the group I had kept asking me to do the unthinkable. Portland is a town full of water ways and big bridges and hills and curves everywhere. It was a group of striking steel workers, and they wanted to use me and the bus as a getaway car for questionable activity surrounding the nice homes of some of the steel industry's more prominent executives. Then they wanted to have me shuttle them around at 2am . . . and be up again at 6am. I guess, before I left them stranded, they decided they would get rid of me, so they called my boss in Colorado. Luckily, John was out in that area coincidentally visiting with family, . . . so he was called in to replace me. I cushioned back to Colorado to safety, narrowly escaping a lynching. A week later, I was assigned to go west on the Grand Junction run. Again, what a coincidence: as I drove into the setting sun, who was coming back from Oregon? but the charter group who thought they'd gotten

me fired. I just smiled and waved--playing
chicken would've been a little much, since John
was a good friend.

Oh, one more driver worth mentioning, Mr
Lange: I never knew him really, and I forgot his
first name, but I cushioned with him once or
twice between Albuquerque and Grand Junction.
Mr Lange was and maybe still is . . . the smooth-
est and most-precise shifter I've ever witnessed.
I thought I was good with those seven-speed
MCIs from the mid 1990s, and I always got nice
compliments from the passenger, after I got the
hang of it--I even had to "float gears" a couple of
times when I received buses where the clutch had
just gone bad. . . . But Mr Lange, oooh, he was
more like a Swiss clock--it was spooky, almost
like he was a Stepford Bus-Driver. I noticed his
run too: he had arguably the most-difficult
shifting run in the West, over 11,000-foot Red
Mountain Pass and two more passes almost as
high, between Durango and Montrose. The thing
that struck me was: you've got more than a couple of hours of 35-mph and even 15- and 20-mph
driving in there with lots of hard climbing and
tight turns and just as much nerve-racking downhill with the real potential threat of having a
runaway. I know how difficult a road it is because I drove a couple of charters over it myself.
The thing you've got to realize is: we were getting paid by the mile, and, with his seniority in
the company, he could have easily had a faster-
sailing higher-paying run--I think he just flat-out
took the most pride in his shifting. He drove that
road six days-a-week for a number of years, north
one day and south the next. Or maybe it could be
he chose that life-threatening route as an atonement for some mistake he had made as a younger

driver--I don't know; but I do know he was the best shifter for that route.

So I nominate Mr Lange as the Greatest Gear-Jammer Ever. I nominate Joe Haley for Greatest Line-Haul Driver Ever. I nominate John Elliot for Greatest Charter Driver Ever. And I nominate Neil Byrne for the Greatest OTR Bus Boss Ever. These are my idols in the Over-the-Road Bus Business.

Other Bus Types

Of course, line-haul drivers, charter drivers, and school-bus drivers don't cover the whole spectrum of bus drivers. There are other types, but they are either a smaller percentage of the whole business, or they are less romantic.

Probably the closest ones to charter drivers are the tour-bus drivers for the famous country-music sangers. I have never done this, but I know a few who have. And you can kind of picture what they're life would be like--it would depend greatly on who they are hauling, to set the tone for the driver. Back in the 1950s, '60s, or even '70s, groups like Asleep At the Wheel probably still drove their own buses themselves, and it was like a big family. Movies like *Honeysuckle Rose* and *Pure Country* show an idea of the atmosphere of these buses--they are Recreation Vehicles with regular homes inside them, instead of a bunch of rows of seats with a restroom. I like what Merle Haggard says to prospective country-music stars: "What it is . . . is a thirty-five year bus ride."

. . . Then you might have a minor-league baseball team traveling in a team bus. I got a kick out of the coach or manager, when Michael Jordan tried minor-league baseball and wasn't happy with his team's bus, so he bought them a new one. The coach or manager was reported to have said, "We had a good bus before; he didn't have to buy us a new one." You can see a bus like this in movies like *Bull Durham* and *A League of Their Own*. I like the scene where the bus driver can't take some of the passengers' antics anymore: he pulls over and parks on the shoulder of the highway, and leaves them without a driver--this kind of scene has probably happened more than you think.

In fact, subbing the line-runs, every now and then, I would get a truck driver who had parked his eighteen-wheeler somewhere and quit his driving job because of being fed-up with some-thing about his employer. Of course, I had to haul the other driver going to rescue that truck too. The same is true of bus drivers, as we've seen in my own personal stories. **You get to a point where you're not going to take any crap from anybody--probably none of my school-bus colleagues understands why I'm so strict and such a hard-ass with kids, parents, outside mo-torists, coaches or teachers or chaperones, ad-ministrators, and other bus drivers.** It's a matter of principle, and those who stand up for right and wrong have over the years become the mi-nority. (Here in 2009, that is starting to change, as evidenced by Susan Boyle's great singing voice . . . and books like this one.)

A high percentage of big buses, starting in the maybe the early 1990s, are casino buses. Besides some smaller-to-medium-size luxury vans, these are the same types of buses as the big-company charter and line-haul buses. Most people don't notice it, but, by the mid 1990s, there were lots of casinos sprinkling the country, almost strategi-

cally located, within a half-day's drive from anywhere in the country. A high percentage of senior citizens were targeted to ride these buses and
pour their money into the nickel slot machines--
the smaller the bet, the higher the percentage the
casinos would keep. I drove for a company
named Ramblin' Express out of Pueblo for thir-
teen months just before my big over-the-road
twenty-four-state career with TNM&O Coaches.
In the one year I was with them, I noticed they
went from a half-dozen tired twenty-year-old
forty-foot MCIs . . . to more than a dozen brand-
new forty-five-foot MCIs. The destination casino
in Cripple Creek was owned by the dad, and the
bus company supplying transportation was
owned by the young son. The month I started,
the bus ride was practically free from Pueblo or
Colorado Springs, and they even gave each passenger five-dollars in free quarters and a free-
meal voucher; in less than a year, they were able
to charge a substantial fee. It was amazing how,
in such a short time, they got so many people
hooked on gambling. As a driver, I got the "free"
quarters and the free meal, but I noticed how
some casino manager often gave me the evil eye .
. . for wandering around but not losing much
money.

I used to joke with the old folks out of Pueblo,
how they could make a good living just riding
the casino buses. They could get on the 6-am in
Pueblo, arrive at Cripple Creek around 8-am,
have breakfast with their meal-voucher and win
some money with their "free" quarters, ride the
10-am down, catch the 2-pm up again for another
meal and more winnings, take the 6-pm down,
have plenty of time to catch the last bus up at 9-
pm for another free meal around 11-pm or 12-

midnight and a third five-dollar chance to win till catching the last bus home at 2-am. So the bus would arrive back down in Pueblo about 4-am, so they had less than two hours before catching the 6-am up again. I told them: "Think about it: you could sell your house and car and everything; you can sleep on the bus, with my smooth driving, and the only time you would have to fill is from about 4:15-am to 5:45-am, a measly hour-and-a-half where you could just go across the street the Denny's for coffee." I swear, there were some old folks who just about lived that way.

One time, I had two old ladies on my casino bus sitting in the right front seat talking about their grand-kids. It seems some drug dealer was offering them free drugs on the play-ground. They went home and told their Grandma, and the Grandma turned around and advised them, "Don't take those 'free' drugs! because that's how they get you hooked!" Little did Grandma know . . . she had fallen for the same scheme . . . in the world of casino-gaming . . . with regard to her retirement checks.

There was one exception to the normal losers on those casino buses. There was one mild-mannered gentleman who usually rode the 9-pm up and who always seemed to come home a winner. Then, one day, I opened up the Sunday Pueblo Chieftain, and there he was, his picture on the "MOST-WANTED" page, among the rapists and murderers--he had found a way to cheat the slot-machines, and they were slow catching on.

It was interesting driving casino-owned buses, but I always noticed: they never knew, as far as a good driver it concerned, when it came to the big buses, they were in the transportation business.

I had some fun times with Ramblin' Express. The last month I was with them, we had a driver meeting. On the way to the meeting, I heard on the early morning radio . . . that legendary country-music sanger Conway Twitty had just passed away. When I got to the meeting, they introduced a new driver, an older fellow who had driven elsewhere for umpteen years. "Hey, you guys, I want you to meet Darwin So-n-So," announced the dispatcher. I couldn't resist stating the obvious, in a soft low voice: . . . "Hello, Darwin." . . . Even the people who hate me . . . can't help but love me sometimes.

. . . Anyway, other than that, you have a handful of drivers driving church buses occasionally, or hauling white-water raft trips for the summer, that kind of thing. This type of deal is a good home for old school buses and even old OTR motor coaches--although I am afraid today's 45-foot bell-n-whistles tour buses may end up being too high-tech for a small church even when the bus is 20-years-old.

I drove a Fire-Crew Bus one summer for Apache and Navajo and Zuni Indians in Arizona and New Mexico. That was somewhat interesting, as we drove on old logging roads quite a bit, and it was not for the faint of heart. I believe, I am proud to say, I got to see places on their reservation lands . . . that no white man had ever seen before.

Oh, I should briefly mention **my very first bus-driving job ever, before I thought of myself as a school-bus driver**. It was the Summer of '82, not to be confused with the *Summer of '42*, in Glacier National Park, I drove a fourteen-passenger 1936 White with a canvas roof you could roll back so the tourists could stand up and take pictures.

I remember, in order to get the job, I was sort of quiet about not yet being able to drive a stick; so, when I got there that first afternoon, I quickly revealed my little secret to a couple of second-year drivers, and they promptly took me out and taught me just in time to meet my new boss the next morning.

Driving mainly back and forth over the treacherous "Going-To-the-Sun" Highway, with Logan Pass, we were known as "Jammers," and we were a cocky but-prestigious young-n-rowdy bunch. Not happy with the dormitory situation, most of us preferred to camp-out in the back baggage compartment of our assigned bus, grizzly bears and all. Our supervisor's main mantra was: "Remember, eight hours between bottle and throttle." We got our unsuspecting passengers for a couple of hours at a time from the big tour buses coming through, which were too big for the pass, so they would dead-head around on US Route 2 and meet us on the other side. One scary thing about that job, if your assigned bus was down with mechanical problems, you were laid-over in East Glacier waiting for it to be fixed, and you didn't work--so there was lots of incentive to cover-up your bus's needs for repair. We got away with a lot in those days: some drivers would even fill an old whiskey bottle with soda-pop or tea to put on an act that would sure give the tourists a scare. Some drivers, the last week of the season, would pretend life was sooo miserable, "recently losing their girl-friend" and all, they would desperately end up parking the bus, passengers and all, and run over to a popular forty-foot high cliff-jumping area . . . where they would pretend they were committing suicide into the icy water below--they would climb back up and emerge sopping wet a minute-or-two later and climb back into the bus laughing . . . to finish the last mile or so of the trip. I never got that wild, as my antics were more subtle, like pointing out the occasional runaway buses at the bottom of the valley.

Legend has is it, back in the '60s or '70s, a half-dozen or more Jammers got to partying one night, they commandeered a bus . . . and took it up Logan Pass . . . and accidentally took a short-cut down three-thousand vertical-feet to there untimely deaths.

I saw a program on Glacier Park recently on the Discovery Channel--low and behold, my Bus #87 was still going strong. When I was driving it, once a week or so an old man would come along claiming to have driven Bus #Such-n-Such way back in 1950-something or earlier. "Yeah," we'd tell him, "your bus is still going strong, . . . but there's a girl driving it now," and a big smile would come over his face. . . . I'd like to take this moment to say hello to some of the Jammers I've never forgotten since that summer more than twenty-five years ago: Katy Killeen, Elin Larsen, Bob Hong, Folsom, Franzen, Rick Squires, Jerry Kariniemi, Jack Curtiss, Director John Hansan, and three more friends, Lynski Fagan, Karna Lamb, and Julie Wong.

One more bus type that I don't know too much about, and maybe don't want to know: prison-inmate buses, maybe like the one in the Harrison Ford movie, *The Fugitive*. Depending on the prisoners, I think they have to drive with more scary policies and procedures than the general public might be aware of, concerning the inmates' freedom of access to emergency doors and so on in case of an accident or a fire. I hope you never see me on a prison bus, and I hope I never see you there either, I think. But, if I ever do end up riding a prison bus as an inmate, I'm confident that, with this book out, I'm sure I could persuade the driver into letting me take the wheel for a few miles.

Speaking of prison inmates, I used to pick up a lot of "graduates" from the penal systems, or travelers "checking out of the Grey Rock Hotel," around Canon City, Colorado, on the regular line runs. They were always escorted to the bus-stop by prison guards, and they always had the identifiable fresh new set of issued clothes. I always took pride in how important the bus driver's role could be, as he has a huge hand in their smooth or rough reentry into society, whether or not a newly-released inmate could end up right back in jail within his first few hours out as a free man: a relaxed and confident driver could help put them at ease and make them fee welcome in the outside world, while a grumpy too-strict driver might drive the ex-con over the edge, causing him to go bad and break the law again. Sometimes you had to orchestrate where some of the other passenger might sit or behave, whether it be a vulnerable 16-year-old girl or a prejudiced old man. You never knew how long they'd been in for, and you didn't know what their crime was--but it made you wonder. And you always wondered, just because they are now free, do they have a home to go to? do they have a job when they get there?-- you have to feel for them, and hope they make it.

City bus drivers don't need much mention, as the most romantic one of this bunch was probably Ralph Cramdon, Jackie Gleason on *The Honeymooners*. Did you notice how stressed out he was all the time?--it didn't all come from Norton. Oh, while I'm thinking of it: I nominate Ralph Cramdon's wife as the Greatest Bus-Driver Wife Ever-- "Baby, . . . you're the greatest." . . . The city-mode of bus driver is probably looking for more security and convenience than the other drivers. He gets a forty-hour week, higher pay than school-buses, there's never a change in plans, and he gets off work the same time every day, and he's home every night--pretty boring. When I looked into a job like this once in Pueblo, Colorado, just before my OTR career, they had a part-time deal where the part-timer made half-as-much per hour compared to a full-timer--ridiculous! absurd! on top of boring!

That's what half of this book is about: trying to find a happy medium. Instead of working your ass off sixty-hours a week, probably making more money than you need, they don't want you to work twenty hours a week, thus keeping twenty others for yourself, making just what you need. So the real workers get overworked, and the moderate workers can't get a fair deal. **SLAVERY** is all it is, and those in charge of making the decisions shrug their shoulders and claim the decisions are handed down from outer-space-- Then they raise the prices so that the sixty-hour-a-week guy barely gets by, and they market low-paying part-time jobs as "making extra money," like you already have enough. This book . . . is how I'm making my "extra money."

Oh, hey! Wait! There's one more type of coach I need to mention, and one more professional driver: the Wells Fargo Stagecoach and a friend of mine named Robin Wiltshire, from Australia. He's the main guy you see in that extravagant stagecoach advertising campaign for Wells Fargo Bank, with the six-horse team, rivaling the old Marlboro Cigarette ads. At the rate our planet is going, I wouldn't doubt it if one day in the future . . . we have to revert back to getting around with horses, . . . as well as refurbished old mountain bikes--a little bicycle can only carry so much, like one person and some gear (--see my *Heinsian BIKE-PACKING* manual), so the horses will have to carry the big loads. I've known Robin Wiltshire since the early 1980s, when I was wrangling dudes in Jackson Hole country, and I have to tell you: he's one of the greatest horsemen in the world--he does those incredible Clydesdale ads for Budweiser Beer also, which you see during the Super Bowl. He didn't come over here from the Great DownUnder on a boat or a plane: I believe he's the first-n-only guy to navigate the oceans . . . via stagecoach. . . . I nominate Robin Wiltshire as the Greatest Stagecoach Driver Ever.

I'm tired, . . . so let's park all the buses . . . and try to wrap this up. It wouldn't hurt to do a post-trip inspection on these big commercial buses, though you won't go to jail if you don't. Take eight hours off--no, make that ten--get yourself a nice hot bath, or at least a long shower, . . . and I'll see you tomorrow for the last chapter.

School-Bus Drivers From Many Walks of Life

A lot of people in this country have talked for decades about staying away from stereotypes and things of that nature. Yet have you ever noticed there are some groups of people who try to perpetuate their own stereotypes, consciously or subconsciously? Traveling around most of our country and living in many different states, moving back and forth many times, I have noticed some of these groups with . . . what you might call . . . a common Over-Soul--it's like maybe they all have the same destiny. You see one set of 6-o'clock newscasters and reporters in one American City, and then you see another set in another big city, and you get the impression they could easily trade places, and nothing much would be different. When you look at the rest of the Animal Kingdom, you notice that one coyote is pretty much like another, one mountain lion is pretty much like another, one beef cow is pretty much like another. Even house cats, you can go around and find another cat that has the identical markings to some other cat you've seen. You see people in the city traffic jams, and they all have the same types of cars or SUVs, and they all have the same hectic lifestyle, with a lot of the same problems. The Hippies of the '60s all had pretty much the same style. Most politicians look the same, and, when movies are made about them, the movie-makers almost have to stick with the stereotypes. I'm not saying it's right or wrong, it's just an observation, that there may be big groups of people . . . with one common over-soul. The huge mythology surrounding the Great American Cowboy sitting alone on his horse on the horizon in the middle of nowhere . . . is in part so successful . . . because it's an attempt to get away from the stereotypes and clones we see in other groups of people; but even the Cowboy Culture has succumbed to this modern-day stereotyping and the need for almost everyone to put everything into nice neat boxes. The Cowboy Culture is full of its old worn-out clichés, like "riding for the brand," as if every brand out there is worth riding for. . . . I know, from personal experience, the more individualistic you are, the harder it can be to fit in.

But, when you start to look at a national grouping of school-bus drivers, you start seeing that there is more an endless number of possibilities, with all the nooks and crannies they fill. Compared to other occupations, school-bus drivers often have half their lives still belonging to their-self. As long as they know their job, and the idiosyncrasies of their own particular place, they are not quite as easily subjected to the homogenization and pasteurization and sterilization you find in other occupations and lifestyles.

One time, hauling a group of Colorado Springs middle-schoolers to Denver for the day, I couldn't help listening to two or three teachers and their students up front talking about who their favorite celebrities and movie stars were . . . and who they would like to be like if they had a chance. I couldn't help but put my own two-cents-worth in: "I don't want to be a famous movie star," I revealed, "I just want to be a guy they make a movie about." The teachers just rolled their eyes in front of the students like that was the dumbest thing a bus driver could possibly say--and I guess I didn't fit their mold of bus-driver.

Again, I want to emphasize I don't intend for this book to start a bunch of witch hunts for bad bus drivers, nor generate a bunch of new red tape in the name of safety. I just wish to help make the whole school-bus driving profession more respectable and warm and human inside and out . . . and make it more desirable for more people to want to enlist as school-bus drivers. There shouldn't be such a long shortage of drivers, as work like this is very honorable . . . and should be more enjoyable.

Many SBDs Lead a Double Life

What a lot of non-driver people don't understand is why School-Bus Driver? Too many people think the only reason you're driving a school bus is because you're not smart enough or talented enough to do anything else. People who are especially deep into the system, with high-ranking jobs at the top of the school system or a big corporation--they are often-times stuck in a way, afraid to speak the truth about what really goes on for fear of rocking the boat and so on, and they probably won't admit that most of their life could be a big fat lie. These "important people" have the nicest homes and the newest cars, with paid holidays and full-benefits, and they don't want any trouble coming in to upset their cozy life-style--it's easier to smile and say "yes" even when you don't mean it, and they expect the same from the people they deal with. A school-bus driver, on the other hand, if he doesn't like something, he can pick up his marbles and find another game a few days later--they always need drivers, and they usually need them now. Anyway, the part-time simplistic school-bus drivers . . . and the complicated overworked aristocrats . . . don't tend to mingle with each other very often--the aristocrats think they are too good to mingle with the commoners, . . . and the school-bus drivers wouldn't want to hang around with people like that anyway, and rightly so.

It's in the Administration where you find the occasional embezzlers; I don't think I've ever heard of a school-bus driver embezzling--I got a lot of lunch-money tips from the kids, but I wouldn't call that embezzling (just kidding). In fact, as I put the finishing touches on this book, I saw on the news where a Phoenix School Principal was in hot water for embezzling. Then, even more fun, his female Assistant Principal was just let go . . . for moonlighting as an "Escort." I guess everybody's just trying to make ends meet the best way they know how. By all accounts, she was a fine Assistant Principal. No word about how good an escort she was, . . . or still is.

I was delighted recently, however, to find out that Dubois, Wyoming, High School had as their keynote speaker for graduation this spring . . . a school-bus driver. That's just over the hill from where I was first so-well trained, interestingly enough. Unfortunately, for too many years, success stories like this have been more the exception than the rule.

For the record, most non-pro drivers might not know this, . . . but a percentage of your OTR semi drivers, probably more-so than bus drivers, have college degrees, . . . including Masters Degrees, PhDs, and

Doctorates. These drivers used to be deep in the system and had jumped through more hoops than they care to remember; finally one day, fed-up with the way things have turned out in their chosen profession, they say, "Heck with it," and they hit the road for change of pace and a simpler kind of life. They are not like most part-time school-bus drivers though, as they tend to need more money, money like they were used to making when they were deep in the system; and they maybe grew tired of the home-life--since probably their kids are grown, maybe their wife left them, or something like that.

So it's kind of like the waiters and waitresses you might see in Los Angeles or New York or in a ski town or an artsy place like Santa Fe--they have big dreams and plans with their creativity, but they need a simple paycheck for now, since they maybe haven't arrived yet. In my six years as an over-the-road bus driver, I don't know how many times I wanted to spill an ice-cold soft drink or a hot cup of coffee in a difficult customer's lap. Some of us don't want a whole new complicated career marching to someone else's drum-beat; . . . and we resent it when the hoop-jumpers resent us for not having to jump through all the same hoops they trained so hard to jump through--I don't even make my dog jump through hoops, and she's the Greatest Dog In the World. . . . So part-time school-bus driving is attractive to these creative entrepreneurial types--it doesn't take but a couple of weeks to get started, and it gives them at least half their work week back . . . to do as they please, to be productive in their own creative way. School-bus driving is done by many walks of life--notice I don't say "all" walks of life, because not all can have the knack for this important job,--and each walk of life can bring something unique and worth-while to their particular school bus.

A part-time school-bus driver could be any one of the following fun professions: horse-trainer, barrel-racer, ski-instructor, painter, sculptor, team-roper, bi-cycle mechanic, old-car restorer, hunter, fishing guide, rock-shop owner, freelance writer, gardener, farmer, rancher, horse-shoer, web-site designer or manager, the list goes on. . . . Moderation has been the key to a lot of balanced lives. Twenty-hour-week drivers have more of a chance of having a home-life, with a spouse, or maybe a dog and cat. Part-time school-bus drivers-- what they give up in security, they gain in flexibility, . . . and hopefully opportunity.

Only here in early 2009, life is getting more-n-more difficult by the day, . . . because the politicians and scared business-people and metaphysically-weak red army ants have allowed this careening train to con-tinue. That's been what's so wrong with the system: they either want you working your ass off in the "gov-ernment-created job" (digging a hole one day . . . and then filling it in the next), or they don't mind if you're living on welfare, making that other guy have to dig even faster, while making the politicians seem more important.

After 9/11, suddenly being a fire-fighter became a bit more respectable, as did being a police officer--they became almost glamorized, with huge billboards of their hardworking faces all over the metropolitan highways. No such thing has happened yet for school-bus drivers, and I certainly don't think we need a global tragedy to get everybody's attention. I'm con-tent that we can stick with cold-n-flu commercials. Just read this book, and pass it on to someone else--that ought to be enough. But always keep a copy for yourself; keep it on your dash-board--that way, when people show you disrespect, hold this book up to their face just like you would hold a cross up to a vampire like Count Dracula, like Bud holds that make-up mirror up to the Mayor's face in the movie *Pleasantville*, possibly one of the top-ten most important movies of all time in the History of mankind.

Again, I don't claim to be the Greatest School-Bus Driver Ever; this honor ought to be bestowed upon every regular route driver and substitute, as every school child ought to think their own bus driver is the greatest, much like they know their Mom is The Greatest Mom In the World. I don't know when or if I'll drive again, but I feel a connection to all school buses out there--it's comforting to think I belong to some kind of Fraternal Order of School-Bus Drivers. Sometimes, when I'm on the sidewalk . . . and a school-bus passes by, I've been known to stop and salute. I've moved around a lot my whole adult life, and I've felt homesick most of the places I've been; I've never been married, and I've never had kids--driving school buses has been my way of trying to plant roots. But it doesn't seem to be my lot in life to stay in one place too long, and this book and my others are the closest things to what you might call . . . my kids. It's like I wish I could be a part of every route, . . . so I package everything I know about the subject in this book--"my routes are planted here." It's been a hard trip for me up until now, but I'm finally feeling like I've found my niches-- no, let me say that another way: I've always known my niches; but, up until recently, before my books really got out, hardly anyone else knew my niches--I feel like "I'm finally getting my parking sticker validated." . . .

And now, with regard to the school-bus side of my life, I feel like I need to find someone soon who I can lateral the football to.

How about . . . An Annual Award?--

For **The Greatest School-Bus Driver . . . Anywhere In the Country**. This award could be given by the President of the United States. Naw, he's too busy with bigger problems and projects, just like I am. It could be given by the State School-Bus Advisory Boards, with the help of the common people in all the nooks and crannies of our great nation. All you have do is go out and find them and recognize them--they're out there. There are extraordinary people driving school-buses, and there other life can be quite a story in itself. The skills they have in there other life very often are beneficial to their school-bus driving. We need some new role-models besides the same old spoiled dysfunctional Hollywood celebrities and over-paid out-of-control sports heroes--not all are bad, but too many are; we need to start looking up to people who are more down-to-worth. Remember, when a famous actor portrays a fine good character in a movie, the actor may get most of the credit, laughing all the way to the bank--even the actors who play the villains get more credit; . . . we need to remember to give credit to the fine human being who lived the exemplary life in the first place.

One reason I thought of this idea is . . . Lyndon Baines Johnson started an annual Small Businessman of the Year Award back in the '60s. --It just so happens, the first man to win that award was my Mom-n-Dad's employer, Berkley Bedell, the pride of Spirit Lake, Iowa, the largest lake of "Iowa Great Lakes"--you've heard of my hometown company: *Berkley's*, with the red heart for a logo, making fishing and marine products that could reel in Blue Marlin out in the Pacific Ocean or down in the Gulf of Mexico. Four out of six in my family worked for Berkley's, and everyone hoped I would to, only I had to go to college where I could ski--my big sister and I were the hold-outs, . . . only she ended up at Honeywell and its predecessors in Phoenix ever since I can remember, which is pretty much the same as working at Berkley's, in my book. Berkley's has kept in its employ a few hundred people ever since I can remember. He became a U.S. Congressman sometime around 1970 for a couple of terms.

But, because of Berkley's, they burned me out on fishing by the time I was 4-years-old--I can honestly say I've caught one fish in my whole life, a blue-gill out of Center Lake, after several hours of waiting . . . and waiting. . . . *Great Lakes Airlines* comes from my hometown too, come to think of it--you may have seen them flying their nineteen-passenger planes around the West. Those glossy Victory Motorcycles, rivaling Harley-Davidson, is the newest success story from my hometown. And Polaris has a factory close by. I guess I felt like my destiny has more to do with Spirit Man than Mechanical Man or Tribal Man. Bless the factory workers' heart, but not all of us can do it. The greatest school-bus drivers are doing a part-time job many wouldn't be caught dead doing, and usually without the higher pay and full benefits, so they deserve more credit.

Business is fine as a priority in this country, but not if we run over school children to get to work. I imagine a lot of the people that do the occasional running over our kids are people just trying to get to work on time . . . or the next job, to make their huge mortgage payments or their high monthly car payments. A lot of your most aggressive drivers are those subcontractors with a new pick-up full of expensive tools, driving around like maniacs on the outskirts of town knowing they need to "bring home three buffalo by the end of the day" (as Stuart Wilde would say) in order to survive--just look in your rearview mirror.

It's no secret that our country and this little world of ours are currently facing some unprecedented major challenges, not just on the horizon, but right under our feet, right under our nose--concerning our food supplies, our energy resources, people's artificial-money predicament, and--I know this one isn't going to win any popularity contests, but--probably over-population. **Not all of us can afford to join the forced march orchestrated by a greedy few.** My different lifestyle of trying to find a balance by teaching skiing most winters, wrangling horses most summers, driving school-buses when I could, writing books in my "spare time," but getting caught in the rapid current of over-the-road buses for several years . . . has been highly put down by most of my family and friends and acquaintances. I can feel their resentment when they criticize me for not slipping into slavery as far as they have. <u>Someone has to take the time to stop and think . . . about the Meaning of Life, . . . not just work their ass off and buy the pre-packaged version of the Meaning of Life that some-selfish-one else has given us and "guaranteed" to be The Truth.</u>

As Human Beings, we seem to have forgotten long ago, . . . that doing your daily chores for yourself . . . is work, that cooking and cleaning for yourself and roofing your own house . . . is work. Someone's got everybody brainwashed into thinking that work is . . . somewhere else . . . out there . . . away from home . . . working more hours in the week . . . than will allow you to get your own chores done at home. When people finally get sick of trying to keep up with the rat-race working for someone else in the private sector, . . . they set their sites on landing a cushy government job-- but again: it's like Multi-Level-Marketing, as eventually the Pyramid Scheme ends up too top-heavy or up-side-down . . . and will topple over. --I cannot be the only one who sees this!

Here, Now, in the middle of 2009, since late in 2008, the System as we know it . . . has started to Collapse. Even many of the secure slave jobs that have been created for us . . . are disappearing fast. While more and more of us individuals can finally take the time to ponder the Meaning of Life, we may need a part-time job to help us get through, if we are not already balanced enough to be moderately self-employed. But, no, the Powers-That-Be can't let you have a happy medium; they either want you working your ass off with no time to think, or they want you discouraged enough to fall into the Welfare State, thus making the hard-workers work even harder. Are we going to try to restore The Old System that got us in this mess in the first place?--all the smartest economists in the world couldn't sort that one out. And, even if they did, the Powers-That-Be wouldn't go along with it.

We need our Spirit back, and fast. This business of working your ass off five or six days a week and then using the other one or two to recuperate . . . has never made sense to me--who came up with that? Working full-time every other day makes more sense; or working five or six half-days a week is moderate; or working Monday-Tuesday, Thursday-Friday, with Wednesdays and Weekends off could be a balanced life, so that a guy has time to enjoy the chores at home. It's like Jack Palance points out in City Slickers: everybody spends fifty weeks a years getting knots in their rope, and then they spend the two remaining weeks trying frantically to untie them. It takes more than a measly two-weeks-a-year to find Balance . . . to understand Truth . . . and be able to Love. Otherwise: what are we?--lemmings off a cliff?--I hope not.

. . . Let's slow down a little bit, . . . on purpose, . . . before Nature does for us. We have everything we need . . . to create jobs . . . and make a living. There's enough work for everyone, if we spread it around and keep Greed in check--and keep our government in check. Let's use our Imagination . . . to live a more Quality Life, . . . instead of seeing how fast we can make life go. School buses could set the new more-natural pace. It wouldn't hurt a few high-level corporate executives to take their turn at school-bus driving. School kids learn from so much more than just their school teachers; they learn from everyone and everything around them--everything. Let's make all necessary work honorable, even school-bus driving, . . . instead of fabricating unnecessary busy-work that's just designed to control people. "The hand that rocks the cradle rules the world," whether it's the child's real mom . . . or some expensive hired day-care worker; . . . and then, before and after kids see their official teachers, they see their school-bus drivers--the hand that steers the wheel rules the world a little bit too. The school-bus gig doesn't have to be the only part-time deal in town; most occupations could be offered with more moderation--if the hard workers could slow down a bit and let some of their work go to the ones who need a hand-up. As Jimmy Buffet sings, "Moderation seems to be the key."

. . . My friend Dan Mortensen, a school-bus driver for twenty-some years, well-balanced in his life with horses as a result, always used to say "Necessity is the Mother of Invention." I didn't want to write this book-- good writing is some of the hardest work I know; and it can take years of your time, and there's no guarantee you'll get paid. But this book is necessary, and that's why I invented it. It's taken twenty-five extra years, a lot of heart-ache, and maybe a million miles . . . to get to this point. There isn't anyone else alive who could have written it--call it **Heinsian Philosophy**. . . . Still, I nominate Dan Mortensen as the Greatest School-Bus Driver Ever.

Here in late July of 2009, as I put the finishing touches on this book, I still don't know what my status is with the current school district I've been subbing for. Because of the historically-hard-new economic times, they are talking about cutting routes and trips and not needing as many drivers--yet we all know they will always need a sub at the last minute. Last year, I had some friction with some coaches on long trips, due to poor planning and lack of respect; and I witnessed a couple of red-light violations with prominent citizens I was obligated to report. Some of the drivers who've never been outside of *Pleasantville* aren't in love with my "more colorful" and thorough approach to the job. Red is part of the job, not just yellow, and Communication is part of the job, whether they know it or not, with just as much gray . . . as there is black-n-white, and my conversations and letters concerning issues are always truthful and frank.   For whatever reason, a power-trip, prejudice, hate, jealousy, I don't know, . . . they are not going to call me in unless they absolutely have to--they can't fire me, because they have nothing to fire me for, . . . but, if I'm a sub, they can sure hold off on calling me in, just like that OTR bus company several years ago did.   Yet the day will come, when they've run out of drivers--one's Mom just passed away, one's got a dental appointment, one just had a heart attack, one just had a grand-child--when they will have to call old Gar'. . . . *Riiinnnng! Riiinnnng! Riiinnnng!* about 4-am in the morning--should I pick up? *Riiinnnng! Riiinnnng! Riiinnnng!* . . . I have a sneaky suspicion that, with the help of this book, they will have lost a good driver, and that will be **The Last Call**. . . . But I also have a sneaky suspicion that, also with the help of this book, they will gain a whole bunch more new ones--it may take a few months, or even years, . . . but they will gain a whole bunch more. . . . I can sleep knowing that.

Well, there it is: a fair amount of black-n-white, more gray than anyone could ever dream, just the right amounts of reds and yellows and every other color necessary to complete this story. If they ever make a movie about all this, . . . I would hope that they don't use an actor any better looking than Yours Truly--we don't want to make it look too good to be true. **The Bus Stops Here.** . . . Check all your mirrors, re-comb your hair if you think you need to, be proud to be a bus driver, . . . and start again . . . at idol speed.

Acknowledgements

Bobbi Anderson, Patti Ashcraft, Vicki Barnett, Donna Brummer, Neil Byrne, JoAnn Camenzind, Otis Connolly, Brandi Davis, Tammy Davis, Dory Dudzik, John Elliott, Patrea Faulkner, Susan Federspeil, Mike Foshee, Manny Garcia, Judy Grant, Joe Haley, Terry Haws, Michelle Johnson, Jeffrey Jones, Mike Killmer, Elton Lee, Andy Lind, Shawna Lockhart, Bear McKinney, Cheryl Martin, Jack McNichols, Dan Mortensen, Rachelle Price, Quannah, Denise Raban, Tim Raban, Helen Scarborough, Katrina, Larry Simmons, Knowles Smith, Cory Vellinga, Crawford Waite, Stuart Wilde, Marianne Wood, . . . and many others.

Hear **what others *might have said*** about
THE GREATEST SCHOOL BUS *DRIVER EVER*
By GARY HEINS

"Yes, I can't go into the details, but Gary Heins was under consideration for Barrack Obama's Senate seat. . . . If he still gets it, would that mean there's a Driver's Seat vacant for someone to fill? Does one have to have a CDL? Would I have to go through a background check? Or how does that work?"

--Rod Blogojovich

"**'The Bus Stops Here'**--huh! sounds like a good line. Fact is: if I hadn't been elected President, School-Bus Driver would have been my second choice--I've already got a Stetson Open Road. If it isn't an elected position, it maybe oughta be . . . or at least a Presidential appointment."

--Harry Truman

"Before this book, when you were a good school-bus driver, I imagine it often felt extremely scary, like being the last human being left in *Invasion of the Body Snatchers*, or at least like Eddie Albert on *Green Acres*."

--Kevin McCarthy

"Heins says most people wouldn't be caught dead driving a school bus. Well, I wouldn't be caught dead driving one either, and I'm a school-bus driver."

--Gary Heins

"Bus-Driving--pretty exciting stuff, Maybe they could make a TV series out of it: . . . Route Patrol."

--Christopher George

"So this Heins fella has written a book about bus-drivin'. What does he think he is? some kind of Road Scholar?"

--*Kris Kristopherson*

"Not only is Gary Heins a great writer, or re-writer, if you know what I mean, but he is also a great re-router---he is re-routing the whole bus-driving industry."

--*James Michener*

"No bus driver . . . in their route mind . . . would pass up reading this book. When cushioning, you can use it as a pillow." --*Unanimous*

"When I'm routin', I'm routin'; when I'm writin', I'm right." --*Gary Heins*

"With his fine books on downhill skiing, getting along with horses, negotiating the western dance floor with a female partner, riding old refurbished mountain bikes, . . . and now School-Bus Driving, . . . Heins, without a doubt, . . . deserves the 'Mobile Prize' for Literature--even Peace, Economics, Physics, Chemistry, and Physiology."

--*Sinclair Lewis*

Watch for **SWINGIN' G BOOKS** n videos
by **GARY HEINS:**

HAVE HARMONY WITH WOMEN
--Heinsian WESTERN SWING

ONE GOOD TURN DESERVES ANOTHER
--Heinsian DOWNHILL SKIING

SIT DEEP IN THE SADDLE
--Heinsian WESTERN RIDING

poetry and friction:

RIMES OF AN ANCIENT SKI TEACHER"
--Heinsian SKI-BOY POETRY

THE GREATEST SKI INSTRUCTOR
IN THE WEST

THE **PROHIBITION**
OF SNOW-BOARDING
By GH--USST

Here are some bonus books:

THE GREATEST SCHOOL-BUS DRIVER EVER

ESCAPE ON TWO WHEELS
--Heinsian BIKE-PACKING

And watch for these columns:

RIDING WITH HEINS-SIGHT
(TWELVE READS)

SKIING WITH HEINS-SIGHT
(FIFTEEN UPRIGHT COLUMNS)

GOLFING WITH HEINS-SIGHT
(--NINE WHOLE COLUMNS)

~~"BUTT-FIRST" WRITING~~
~~--THE HEINSIAN WAY~~
~~(TWELVE INSTILLMENTS)~~

To bring **GARY HEINS** *EXPERT WITNESS* for buses to your area, . . . or to find out his other services, call the *HeinsQuarters* of the:

SWINGIN' G RANCH
PO Box 784
Saint Johns, Arizona 85936
(928) 205-7756

Thanks.   www.wrangler-skier.com

#######

GARY HEINS
circa 1990

at the *HeinsQuarters* of the
SWINGIN' G RANCH